HYGGE

Discovering The Danish Art Of Happiness –
How To Live Cozily And Enjoy
Life's Simple Pleasures

OLIVIA TELFORD

HYGGE: Discovering the Danish Art of Happiness –
How to Live Cozily and Enjoy Life's Simple Pleasures
by Olivia Telford

© **Copyright 2017 by Olivia Telford**

All Rights Reserved.

ISBN-10: 1548283320
ISBN:13: 978-1548283322

ALSO BY OLIVIA TELFORD

The Art of Minimalism:
A Simple Guide to Declutter and Organize Your Life

Mindfulness: The Remarkable Truth Behind Meditation
and Being Present in Your Life

Cognitive Behavioral Therapy: Simple Techniques to Instantly
Overcome Depression, Relieve Anxiety, and Rewire Your Brain

To Hannah, for being my best friend,
for believing in me and inspiring me to write,
and for making me laugh everyday.

CONTENTS

INTRODUCTION

Hygge (pronounced "HOO-ga") is a Danish and Scandinavian concept that describes a personal feeling rather than an abstract concept. In other words, the experience of Hygge is felt within an individual's body and is not just something merely understood by the mind. The boiled-down meaning is "coziness," but the high-level meaning is an approach to living. Hygge embraces the idea of positivity and enjoyment that comes from everyday experiences. Cultivating this type of mindset requires an individual to pay better attention to their mind and surroundings. This idea permeates the core concepts and overall attitudes about life and how people Denmark, and the wider Nordic region, live. This book will focus predominantly on the ways that Danes experience hygge and how other Westerners can also experience it.

Hygge is not merely a noun, but it is also a verb and an adjective. It is a diversified term used to describe a scenario, emotion, and way of life that centers itself on the idea of "being cozy." While this is quite a broad definition, it allows the person who implements it the freedom to decide what it means for them, which is cozy in and of itself. The additional benefit is that the concept is fluid and moldable to anyone's circumstances and preferences because an individual experiences hygge uniquely. In other words, no matter who you are, you can implement and benefit from hygge.

Therefore, anything you decide is cozy and comfortable could be considered hygge. Whether that is soft lighting, a roaring fire, walking around your home naked, cuddling with a loved one, or even the repetitive movements of shaving. If it is something comforting, you can define it as hygge. It also extends outside of the home. It can be walks in nature, feeding ducks at a lake, or going out to eat at your favorite restaurant. Whatever you decide to be hygge is hygge for you. It's not a one-size-fits-all concept, but it is a concept that fits all sizes! Confusing, right? No worries! This book will clear that up.

But if you look at hygge from this particular angle, you'd think it was just an adjective, right? Well, something merely described as comfortable is simply that. However, the word "hygge" is also a noun, and it is derived from the symbolic interpretation placed on an inanimate object or a living person. For instance, if someone walks into an antique shop and finds the atmosphere calming and feels joyful and at peace, that antique shop is hygge for them. That shop is a physical manifestation of an inner feeling they experience when stepping through its doors. In that way, "hygge" is a noun. Certain jewelry, like a ring, could be considered hygge; as could a favorite t-shirt.

However, as stated above, Hygge is also a verb. And in the Danish lifestyle, hygge is a way of life. People who desire Hygge in Denmark actively strive for it every day. In the same way that many Americans strive to stuff in everything they can into each day before they close their eyes at night, Danes focus on hygge to be their lifestyle. Not only is hygge strived for, but other people praise it. In this way, it comprises a positive feedback loop, both internal and external, keeping hygge as a focus even more straightforward.

It sounds like a dream, doesn't it?

So, it is essential to remember that hygge means different things to different people. Throughout this book, you will learn various ways to implement hygge into your life, but it will always be up to you to decide precisely what it means to you. Think of this book as an exploratory guide and not as a set of instructions. Your reading and implementation of concepts in this book should be fun and not a chore, so be sure to bring flexibility and creativity when you implement hygge into your life. Hey, even while I was writing this book, I experienced hygge myself!

Helen Russell, an author and active member of her Danish community, defines hygge as a total absence of things that might annoy you, stress you out, or cause you to become emotionally overwhelmed. She also points out that hygge requires prioritizing people in your life whom you love and feel at ease around.

In other words, her definition is surrounding yourself with things and people that take your stress away and make you feel comfortable. Again, this can mean different things to different people. It also determines everything from what you eat for breakfast, to how you decorate your house, to what scent you decide to put in your car. It means you can decide whether small family gatherings, large gatherings of friends and family, or mostly solitude is hygge-like to you. The best thing with this approach is that you can use hygge to fit your needs or overhaul your personality to fit your new hygge lifestyle. Cool, right?

Americans, English-speaking Canadians, and many other native English speakers have trouble understanding the word "hygge" because it is impossible to translate precisely and accurately. There is no word other than "cozy" to capture the feeling, though many Danes will be quick to tell you that the word cozy lacks the essence of living hygge. The best description I've heard from a Dane translating it to English is: "the enraptured enjoyment of the simple things in life," but even this characterization is lacking. Language has its limitations on expressing individual emotional states, and for hygge, it is no different. However, sometimes using language to highlight an image can be beneficial. Remember those commercials where a family was gathered in front of a fire, sitting around a dinner table packed with their favorite foods, or gathered on the couch enjoying their favorite movie, and the words "ENJOY THE FINER THINGS IN LIFE" would scroll across the screen? Well, that is an excellent foundation to build on when you begin your journey into the hygge lifestyle. You should make sure to enjoy the finer things in life, but not so much that you overindulge. Suppose you find comfort in eating chocolate cake, great! But if you eat a whole cake every day, you're unlikely to feel comfortable in your body due to the adverse effects of eating unhealthily. Hygge is about balance in your life, so pay attention to this balance as much as possible.

It is understandably frustrating to many that hygge does not have a direct translation. But hey—some of the best things this world has to offer defy precise definition. Have you ever heard someone say, "I couldn't even begin to describe how I felt"?

Well, that's similar to hygge. Despite what the term lacks in verbal definition, it makes up for in physical and emotional experiences that produce positive reactions in the body. Even though language is an excellent way to frame experience, it is not always sophisticated enough to define various concepts accurately.

Hygge is such an essential part of the Danish culture and is so innate that they integrate it into their lifestyle with minimal effort. Those 15-minute hot cocoa sessions they give themselves to wind down their day are a defining feature of how they live their life. The relaxation and stress-free environment small rituals like this provide Danes is similar to a quick cup of coffee in a disposable cup is for Americans. These little moments of comfort help brighten up even the darkest of days, making hygge an indispensable tool to facilitate overall well-being.

One reason why I think it's so important to learn from hygge is that Denmark consistently tops the Forbes chart of The World's 10 Happiest Countries. Year after year, it remains within the top three, and many of those years, it inhabits the #1 spot. This success is no fluke, and many Danes proclaim it is the hygge lifestyle that keeps everyone happier. It permeates every aspect of society—rich or poor, male or female, young or old. It is because hygge is so far-reaching and applicable that collectively, regardless of background, the country's population remains happier than most others nearly all of the time.

One of the best parts of living a hygge lifestyle is that it doesn't require a substantial bank account. This lifestyle exists within the confines of what an individual sees as satisfying, stress-relieving, and happiness-inducing. For some, a special scent wafting from the melted wax of a vanilla candle is enough to release enough serotonin to induce what we, as humans, experience as "happiness" and "relaxation." A short jog around the neighborhood might satisfy another person. A few minutes to breathe deeply can induce hygge. Whatever brings you more happiness in your life is likely to help you in your quest to foster a hygge-mindset. And let's face it, many people in this small world of ours could use a little more happiness in their lives.

The principle behind the hygge philosophy sprouts from the seed of 'not doing too much.' Simply put, happiness and stress-relieving environments only exist within small intervals of our existence because we often cram too many activities into our days. Our incessant busy-ness is a self-inflicted poison, but that allows the self-inducement of the hygge-flavored antidote. With a hygge mindset, we can learn to free up more time to give ourselves more comfort. Better yet, we can liberate ourselves from the mentality that work comes before everything else and learn to focus on other things in life that truly matter to us.

Within the hygge lifestyle, you will discover moments of 'hyggelig;' meaning that a specific moment is full of hygge. These moments bring about calm, emotionally stable, and relaxing moods. Perhaps when you sink into a warm bath, you can define the moment as hyggelig. Maybe it's the first time you sit on the sofa after a busy day. When you experience these moments, remember to think of them as hyggelig. Using this type of language will help you cultivate the hygge mindset, which will allow you to draw greater comfort from your day-to-day life, improving your overall well-being.

For many Danes, if you ask them to define "hygge," they won't know what to say. It is like asking Americans to define "optimistic" and why they think it's essential to have energy and enthusiasm for going to work. The idea and concept are so ingrained in the American culture that it permeates our television shows and even our own lives. If someone asked an American to define "optimistic," they might start explaining that it means you act positively at all times. Better yet, ask them why they tend to be so enthusiastic, and they are likely unable to define why. American culture teaches you that you can be or do anything if you put your mind to it. While this is brilliant in some respects as Americans tend to have greater self-confidence than those of other nationalities, it can also be detrimental when Americans over-inflate their abilities through optimism and at the expense of a more nuanced sense of reality.

For Danes, defining "hygge" comes with a similar reaction of uncertainty. In trying to do so, they will likely pause, contemplate, and then try to find the right word or sentence to describe something ingrained in the fibers of their being and beyond adequate description. They might have a "go-to" way of describing what it is, but they will always find it inadequate.

Despite this, Danes do a fantastic job of living the lifestyle and that's the essential part of hygge. Why spend time trying to define something when you could use that time trying to live something? The latter is far more rewarding.

For many Danes, hygge is a form of intimacy. A hygge follower's goal is to create an intentional, intimate surrounding that induces specific chemical reactions within the brain that promote stress relief, contentment, and relaxation. And, as they will make sure to let you know, a follower will induce these reactions purposefully. Creating these atmospheres is paramount for them and is as second nature as going to the bathroom. Some slip in and out of these moments of hygge, but many live this lifestyle throughout their day. Again, it depends on the individual how much hygge they want to fit into every day.

So, instead of continuing to define "hygge," let's take a look at the health benefits that come with living this sort of lifestyle—because there are many that will benefit your life to no end.

It is common knowledge that deep, intentional relaxation and meditation have been known to help with anxiety disorders and depression. It is also common knowledge that stress, left unchecked by personal regulation or a doctor, can lead to sleeping problems, lack of focus and mental acuity, social withdrawal, and many other issues. These issues can compound each other, meaning sleeping problems can worsen anxiety and depression adversely over time, and vice-versa.

However, did you know that the most common ways doctors tell people to relieve their stress are all things found within the hygge lifestyle?

Well, now you do! The top three most recommended methods to use if you are struggling with your stress levels or depression are socializing with people you love and enjoy the company of, getting regular physical activity, and implementing frequent relaxation techniques (such as meditation, deep breathing, or getting a massage). These activities remind an individual that it is within their power to heal themselves and prevent further negativity in their lives.

All of these methods and thousands more fall under the category of living a hygge lifestyle. Is it any wonder that Denmark is so high up on those world happiness charts? Most Americans have to be told by doctors, counselors, and therapists to implement various lifestyle, dietary changes, and techniques to improve their mood. On the other hand, Danes naturally work these techniques into their everyday lives. Once you learn to make positive habits second nature, your life will improve drastically—so make hygge living a positive habit that you seek out as much as possible!

Living a hygge lifestyle encompasses elements of many "cop-out" slogans and platitudes we tend to hear often. It takes a little "don't be so hard on yourself" and wraps it up in a "live a little" blanket before tucking it into bed alongside a healthy dose of "just kick up your feet and relax." These somewhat foreign ideas to the average American of "slow down" and "take it easy" and "do something you enjoy" are all common threads that allow Danish people to be happy and satisfied people. Perhaps you can take comfort that the Western world does pay attention to these concepts sometimes. Look no further than the British poster shown just before World War II that encouraged citizens to "keep calm and carry on" as an example. This attitude is ingrained in Britons, and you can see it everywhere, from mugs to the sides of buses to posters in people's homes.

Danes who follow the hygge lifestyle are not trying to convince you that their lives are somehow perfect. There are plenty of Danes who do not enjoy their jobs, fight with their spouses, or have stress raising their children. What is different about their culture is that they do not accept this feeling of anxiety, worry, and uptightness as an unavoidable part of their everyday lives. They engage in purposeful activities and habits to actively abolish it. They make it a point to "enjoy the finer things in life." They enjoy things that we often dismiss as lazy or self-indulgent. But things like lying down for twenty minutes if it's needed command status within Scandinavian cultures. Because of that, Danes lead happier lives than over 60% of the world's population. The difference then is that when many Americans put their feet up, they feel guilty about not working hard enough. But these moments are fundamental to life's enjoyment, and they should be utilized with balance—no more feeling bad for relaxing. Your body, mind, and soul all need it!

There has to be a way that Danes find happiness within their lives that they swear are just "everyday lives." Because Danish lives can still be full of stress and worry—one moment someone is trying to cook and their child is dumping flour on the floor, another moment a boss comes down on someone else with hard deadlines, and parents expect their offspring to travel long distances for the holidays. So, even by the Western world's definitions, Danish lives are typical in this respect. We can expect to experience similar things.

Yet Danes are happy. Why?

The answer lies within the insight, implementation, and lifestyle of hygge. When you read this book, you will gain and cultivate all these by incorporating hygge into your life.

In this book, you will learn how to implement those moments of hygge and comfort more regularly into your day-to-day. Hygge is not here to change your life; it is here to enhance it. If you're ready for some Danish-style means of self-improvement, you're in the right place.

Welcome, reader, to the reassuring and comforting world of the hygge lifestyle. It is ready for you as soon as you are ready.

JOIN OUR HYGGE GROUP

To maximize the value you receive from this book, join our tight-knit community on Facebook. Here, we focus on sharing experiences to gain more prosperity, abundance, and happiness. It is a safe place to connect and share with other like-minded readers to continue your growth.

It would be great to connect with you there.

Stay well,

Olivia Telford

To Join, Visit:

www.pristinepublish.com/hyggegroup

YOUR FREE GIFT

As a way of saying thanks for buying this book, I'm offering a free eBook that's exclusive to my readers.

With the Minimalist Guide, you'll discover how to be happier with less, declutter, and simplify your life. People who practice minimalism experience clarity, peace of mind, stronger relationships, and true lasting happiness. You too can experience the amazing benefits of becoming a minimalist by getting this FREE eBook now!

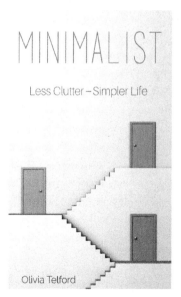

Visit: www.pristinepublish.com/minimalist

DOWNLOAD THE AUDIO VERSION OF THIS BOOK FREE

If you love listening to audiobooks on-the-go or enjoy narration as you read along, I have great news for you. You can download the audio book version of *Hygge: Discovering the Danish Art of Happiness* for FREE just by signing up for a FREE 30-day audible trial!

Visit: www.pristinepublish.com/audiobooks

CHAPTER 1:

WHERE DOES HYGGE COME FROM?

In a technical sense, the word "hygge" derives itself from a Norwegian word meaning "well-being." It first appeared in Danish writings in the 19th-century and has since evolved to encompass an entire cultural phenomenon known most prominently in Denmark. But this definition is just the technical aspect of its linguistic history, though, and every Dane you will ever come across will likely think of every other word in their

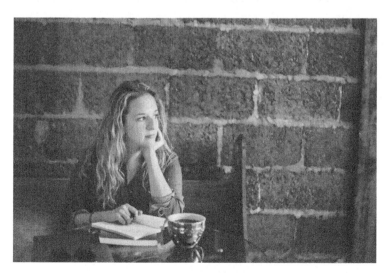

language before deeming hygge "technical." As we explored in the introduction, hygge is an emotional term. It has no specific meaning, but it can encompass all aspects of an individual's life. Its definition isn't apparent in that respect, so let's explore the history of the term and its application.

You may be less interested in where the term "hygge" comes from and more interested in its evolution. For us to consider this, there are a variety of questions we need to ask. How did hygge evolve into what it means today? How do we implement it in our own lives? Does hygge have a specific color, slogan, or mascot? Does it have an enthusiastic following? Does it have a book of directions or a user guide? Does it have rules, regulations, or expectations? How did it come to be in practice?

In Denmark, there are many different factors as to why hygge took off. First of all, their climate is mostly dark and cold, with winter being the longest season of the year, which means that the Danes spend a great deal of time bundled up indoors. So, their lifestyle of hygge has evolved to implement things they can enjoy inside. The limitation of having to be inside has led Danes to be more creative with their living spaces to make them as comfortable as possible, inducing a hygge state of mind. Inside a Danish house you often find what we see in stereotypical pictures: warm socks, soft candles, a roaring fireplace, and a comfortable blanket slung over the knees. But that is merely one person's version of hygge. Other Danes set up their houses somewhat differently, and they also might feel hygge in other moments that have nothing to do with winter at all.

Even though we may think of Denmark as a country full of remote cabins in the wilderness, hygge does not necessarily mean isolation. For Danes who are cooped up during their harsher winter months, life is usually bustling with friends and family. Some evenings Danes bring families and loved ones together. They consume hot food and cold wine over good conversation, share laughter among old friends, and punctuate these experiences with the scent of smoke caused by a roaring log fire flicking its orange and red fingers towards the chimney. Hygge, in this context, is an intimate setting of togetherness that releases stress, frees the mind, and helps folks unwind from the pressures of life. In this context, hygge is social and full of love. The outside may be cold, but the house is full of warmth.

In this particular instance, then, your hygge is more personal rather than directional. In other words, what it invokes in the individual determines whether it is hygge or not.

Hygge is felt in the very being of the person implementing the hygge lifestyle. In American culture, a "lifestyle" often comes with rules and limitations, like a strict diet or a new exercise program. There is a "1-2-3" and a "step-by-step" to the dance of something new. There is a constraining discipline as well as uncertainty. However, a lot of these rules get broken almost before a person begins. If you try to put too many limitations on your life, a part of you will want to rebel, and a strict diet can lead to a binge that may never have happened before the diet was implemented. Because hygge does not have specific rules or instructions, it can be frustrating to understand precisely what it means to you at first. But have no fear, as over time it will become clearer and more apparent as to what hygge means to you.

Remember that the individual is an essential factor in determining hygge because, remember, hygge is felt, not defined.

What Americans may be missing is the conscious part of their awareness in developing hygge in their lives. Once they work out this problem, the implementation of hygge may become second nature. In Denmark, hygge and the idea of carving out times of hygge started as a more conscious pursuit and has taken place throughout their lifetime. It is, therefore, easier for them to implement it naturally. One of the goals of hygge could be to implement it so often that you no longer have to think about it. Hygge may eventually become as simple to you as taking a breath.

Many Americans tend to bring work home with them and respond to the pressure that they think they need to be "always-on" at all hours of the day. However, a Dane will likely spend less time bringing work home and more time with hygge-like family and friend engagements. The reason Danes find it challenging to define and describe its origins to us is because the effort they put into hygge is natural and would likely have been passed down to them culturally since they were born. Just like people make a conscious effort to drive by a coffee shop to grab a steaming cup of latte macchiato, Danes make a conscious effort to carve out slow and intimate moments with people they treasure. If you ask someone to give up their morning coffee run in the US, they might look at you with a dumbfounded expression and laugh off your suggestion. A Dane would react similarly to that suggestion if you asked them to give up their hygge. It is at least a habit that serves them well, and at most a fundamental part of their DNA!

Many people also look at Denmark and see other factors that could contribute to their life satisfaction: they have universal healthcare, free college education, and shorter workdays. Is hygge, then, a way to profit off others and peddle some sort of "item" to purchase? Not exactly. Danes tend to look at the overly stressful consumerist systems—prevalent especially in the US—and wonder why people are not implementing hygge into their lives, which they believe is nothing more than common sense. To Danes, the way Americans run their lives, operate their educational system, construct their workdays, and dole out their healthcare is nothing short of crazy. They chuckle when Americans discuss their ideas about being "progressive" because the same practices are practically ancient for the Danish.

What is essential to understand about the stereotypical perception of hygge is that the pictures we see that are deemed "hygge" are merely manifestations of how hygge is interpreted and represented within one distinct culture. Because the Danish spend a great deal of time in the dark and inside their homes, they always consider the lighting when making a room comfortable and relaxing. Most homes do not have fluorescent lights because the unnatural light can strain eyes, which leads stress-inducing environment rather than a relaxing one. Instead, they are likely to incorporate several lower pools of light that give off a softer, more intimate atmosphere than one massive light up above the head. This is why Danes tend to gravitate towards candles lit in several different places. The additional benefit of this approach is that Danes can use scented candles, adding another layer of hygge to their lighting. You can't exactly have a scented lightbulb!

As the stereotypical winter imagery is associated with the evolution of hygge in one specific culture, many people have come to believe that hygge can only be experienced in the winter, and this is simply not true. Hygge is an emotional, inward, and profoundly personal experience. Because of that, its implementation can be worldwide, year-round, and incorporate any person of any size, shape, color, gender, race, and so on. It doesn't matter the weather, your interests, or whether you like to spend most of your time surrounded by people or alone. Hygge means different things to different people, and it is not discriminatory as you can tailor it to suit your personal preferences.

Even so, the Danish experience up to 17 hours of darkness every single day in the shivering depths of their winters. Their average temperatures hover around 32°F. As they spend more time indoors, the main focus of social interaction is indoors rather than outdoors. Frequent gatherings occur at houses for people to enjoy each other's company, and these types of gatherings take place year-round. However, while the gathering of others might stimulate one person, some people will enjoy and seek the silence that solitude brings.

And that is just fine. Hygge is flexible like that.

One of the cruxes of hygge is 'being kind to yourself.' Although that phrase may be overused, it couldn't be more accurate in the hygge context. Hygge means indulging in something that truly allows you to settle down, quit rushing around your day stressed and anxious, and enjoy what life offers you in more comfortable moments. For some, hygge is a hot tub and a glass of wine. For others, hygge is a late-night binge-watch of their favorite television show. For others, it is dinner and drinks out with friends. And for some individuals, it is wrapping up in a blanket or dancing alone to music. All of these situations can be considered hygge. Not matter what time of day or year, the person—and not the circumstance—always dictates what hygge is. And the circumstance is up to the individual to manipulate to allow them the best possible chance of experiencing hygge.

In Denmark and Danish culture in general, self-enforced deprivation is hardly a thing, especially when compared to Western cultures. Rather than refusing to eat certain comfort foods or refusing alcoholic drinks, many Danes encourage indulging in these luxuries of life rather than abstaining from them. But they do preach moderation, not just infinite consumption. Why? Because low levels of indulgence can lower stress levels and reduce random cravings. Practicing moderation can also prevent overindulgence. Many people believe that allowing oneself consistently to indulge in relaxation will result in obesity. Yet, the highest-dieting country in the world is the United States, and it consistently remains the number one country globally for obesity rates, with a whopping 34% of the population considered morbidly obese.

With its intentional indulging for hygge purposes and comfort, Denmark has a significantly lower 19% of its population classified as obese, with 7% overall considered morbidly obese. This statistic is still a problem, of course, but the Danes have far less of a problem than their American counterparts do.

Therefore, these statistics do not match the countries' frames of mind regarding promotion of indulgence, which you may find ironic.

Let's explore this further.

Just as the prohibition era in the United States saw a significant rise in alcohol consumption, forced restriction causes an overindulgence of foods, libations, and entertainment. When the American government abolished prohibition, alcohol consumption levels began to level out, and the percentage of people treated for alcoholism plummeted. Why? Because there was no longer legally enforced deprivation going on. People had more of a choice, rather than a suppressed desire. If we suppress our urges too much, they can manifest in extreme and self-destructive ways. Therefore, it is essential that we cut ourselves a bit of a break and ensure we live a life of moderation and leeway. Unless it is absolutely fundamental to cut something from your life entirely, like it is for an alcoholic who attends Alcoholics Anonymous and admits they are powerless against the substance, moderation is generally a healthy way to engage in hygge.

There's a basic psychological phenomenon called the "pleasure principle." It is a Freudian concept that hygge feeds off. The idea centers on the fact that our base functions (sex, hunger, thirst, and anger) must always be met. They are the biological basis for any human being. By refusing to fulfill those desires, we breed anxiety, tension, and stress, leading to an outpouring of indulgence in our basic desires. Hygge encourages the idea of indulging in pleasures every day to fulfill those basic urges, so the stress and anxiety never build. When forced deprivation begins to happen, tensions mount, and the idea of "binging and purging" begins to rear its ugly head because the guilt associated with indulging in it can overtake the soul—and this is especially true if the behavior is illegal!

In a state of hygge, the person lives a life that gives the body exactly what it needs but goes deeper than just nutrition. Therefore, for hygge, we should seek to satiate not only our stomachs and bodies but also nurture our souls with high-quality, comfort-inducing food and drink.

Remember, you should feel and experience hygge rather than identify it. The experience of hygge varies from person to person and is partially dependent on what tends to breed anxiety and stress within a particular individual. For some, indulging in a sweet treat at the end of the day can foster a sense of peace. A long walk in the early morning hours to watch the sunrise gives some people the ability to breathe deeply and smile. And for others still, the mere idea of locking themselves away and turning the light off to lay in the darkness is their comfort and makes them feel secure. Neither approach is correct per se, but each approach has the potential to be hygge for any given person. That's the magic of it!

Again, what any person deems hygge depends on how something makes them feel. What one person calls relaxing, another calls a nuisance. What one person considers safe; another considers uninteresting. What one person considers indulgent; another might find disgusting. The beauty of hygge is the beauty of life—every individual is different, and no two experiences are the same.

A way to picture this can be to envision the music you like. Perhaps you like heavy metal, but someone else likes hip hop, whereas someone else likes jazz. Each of these genres could create hygge in specific individuals but could actively work against an experience of hygge in others.

Therefore, hygge is so much more than merely understanding the origins and how it is labeled. It goes way beyond a mere ideal within the Danish culture. The stereotypical images we have associated with hygge and its lifestyle may be elements born out of one particular culture on the planet during a specific time of year, but hygge is more than even the sum of these images. Hygge can span every holiday, season, weekday, hour of the day, geography, and mood. The only thing it is dependent upon is the person implementing the lifestyle, and that lifestyle only has one rule: experience the comfort and safety that life can afford.

CHAPTER 2:

FUNDAMENTALS OF HYGGE

I t can be challenging to understand the fundamentals of hygge because the concept tailors to the individual. It can be even more challenging to pin down the fundamentals because hygge does not have a step-by-step guide. It is the deep-felt necessity of relaxing our souls, allowing us to cast aside our worries and enjoy something that fills a present need for our emotional and mental well-being. However, there are a few things to keep in mind when initiating hygge, no matter the season or the person adopting the lifestyle. Therefore, despite hygge's individualistic nature, you can still use some foundational tools in your quest to develop hygge in your life more effectively.

Although the words "warm" and "cozy" are often overused when discussing hygge, they still fit better than most terms. With hygge, no matter what you are enjoying, comfort and pleasure are paramount. This idea—one that has been trending on social media platforms such as Pinterest and Twitter—has the foundation of nurturing one's emotional and mental well-being. If someone is consciously indulging in hygge, it is imperative to feel these two things. When there is comfort, there is relaxation; when there is pleasure, there is happiness. These two ideals combined create the ultimate bodily conditions for reducing stress and alleviating anxieties, which lowers cortisol levels, leaving the body to rest and heal in ways it so desperately needs. Therefore, the first fundamental in incorporating hygge into your life is to consider what makes you feel warm on the inside and cozy on the outside.

The Danes splice the word "hygge" when labeling things that contribute towards the lifestyle specifically. For example, "sweatpants," or other pants someone would never wear in public but will frequently wear around the house, are called "hyggebukser." The word "hyggelig" is also used relatively often in Danish culture, and this word simply means "hygge-like." Another spliced Danish word is "hyggekrog," which refers to an area of the home where a person can hunker down and relax. These words are spliced with the word "hygge" because they have evolved into Denmark's own "basics" for living, contributing to a hygge lifestyle.

To implement hygge for the first time, you will have to do so consciously. When you navigate through the world, including within your own house, consider what aspects of your day or what areas you feel are the coziest and most pleasurable. Begin to make a mental checklist as to what you think hygge is to you. In these early stages, you could perhaps even write down the things that feel hygge to you. Doing so may reinforce the necessary behaviors for you to implement the lifestyle for your betterment.

While Danes find hygge effortless to employ, other cultures—especially fast-paced ones like American culture—require individuals to make a conscious effort to slow down to really take in life's finer moments and pleasures. Therefore, Americans should employ a "conscious effort" when laying the foundation of a hygge lifestyle. When you get more in tune with thinking about what hygge is and what it isn't, you will likely implement hygge more naturally in your life and will no longer have to make that mental or physical checklist.

When cultures prize speed-of-light communication and hard work over personal well-being and familial connection, a rift can happen among the fundamental aspects of human health: mental, emotional, spiritual, and physical. Food has to be served fast, coffee has to be fast, meetings have to be fast, and work has to be fast. Then, people return home, and television has to be fast, the internet has to be fast, and sleep has to be fast. There is little room for slowing down if you comply too deeply with American and other Western societies' cultural pressures.

These efforts at meeting a perceived "need for speed" only wreak havoc on the body to the detriment of its health. Never slowing down increases the risk of chemical dependencies (such as caffeine) and increases the risk of various health issues. Denmark is the third healthiest country in the world, while countries like the United States and the United Kingdom are among the 10 unhealthiest countries in the world. But why is this the case? Part of the reason is the way the cultures prioritize family and well-being alongside work. If work becomes the top priority, health falls to the wayside. If family, friends, and personal experience become the most important aspects of someone's life, they will likely live healthier and happier lifestyles. It really is that simple.

This is why people in countries that prioritize work over health will need to make conscious efforts at first in order to implement the hygge lifestyle. It requires a refocusing of priorities, a relearning, if you will. If an individual implements hygge for long enough and reaps the scientifically proven benefits, then a conscious effort will no longer be required. But in order to reach this state of unconscious application of hygge, an individual must complete the difficult task of laying the foundation. After all, you can't build a functioning house without a solid foundation, can you?

Another critical aspect of hygge is the application of togetherness—for some at least, because others enjoy spending their downtime alone. Many natural introverts, especially those with chaotic jobs, enjoy coming home and just being alone in solitude. So, while many will say that "togetherness" is a component of hygge, it might not be so for others. The Danish culture has integrated togetherness for various reasons, including having larger families, an emphasis on familial bonding, and the harsh weather they experience, which brings collective enjoyment into the comfort of people's homes, but that does not mean "togetherness" is a requirement for hygge. However, instead of "togetherness," peaceful "enjoyment" is a fundamental aspect of hygge. In other words, if you enjoy your solitude and seek it out more than you seek out group activities, then so be it! Spend more time in solitude and embrace this as a fundamental aspect of your hygge.

In order to be relaxed, comfortable, and content, the person implementing the hygge lifestyle simply needs to enjoy what they are doing. For many, this means gathering friends and family together around a great big table of food while laughing and telling stories. For others, that type of crowd and noise level may increase their worries and stresses, and they might want to be excused as soon as possible so they can go back to their personal spaces and enjoy their version of hygge. And some will even enjoy both of these things and find hygge in social gatherings and solitude!

Remember that solitude is different than loneliness. The former involves self-imposed exile from people in order to decompress, and the latter is a perpetual state of sadness arising from the absence of people someone feels care about them. One has the potential to be very hygge; the other is the exact opposite. If you are lonely, it is great to reach out to people you care about and care about you. This type of reaching out will surely lead you to feel more comfortable and will allow you to experience hygge more easily. Therefore, fundamentally, hygge can be the presence of people or the absence of people. It all depends on how you feel.

In order to understand the fundamentals of hygge, it is crucial to understand what hygge is not. Hygge is not something you must feel compelled to do at all costs, especially to the point that it bothers you if you are not engaging in something you consider hygge. If it feels forced or required of you in some fashion, you will likely not feel relaxed or comfortable—thus defeating the primary purpose of a hygge lifestyle in the first place. Just like a homework assignment is required, or the due date for a paper is mandatory, that will induce stress. Even if you want something as simple as a meal with a specific calorie count, that meal can become stressful. Something as basic as choosing what to eat can be just another thing that you have to remember and measure out to the point of stress. Remember that too many self-imposed rules will not allow you to feel hygge and will likely be detrimental to your overall wellbeing. Even what would have otherwise been a "relaxing" family dinner can become yet another block of time that you spend feeling stressed.

Therefore, you must look at hygge as something you choose to do, and never as a requirement. You should intentionally seek it out for the purpose of goodness, comfort, and coziness, and give yourself a break if you think you're doing something that isn't "hygge-like."

Other ways to experience hygge are to get out and experience something entirely new. Many people find hygge within adventures and thrill-seeking activities, but they may not have realized these things were hygge for them until they tried them out. Part of hygge is not only falling back onto things you understand about yourself; it is also about discovering aspects about yourself you did not previously know. Maybe you will take that hike up the mountain and realize it's not your cup of tea, but now you know for sure. Perhaps you will decide to take your best friend and go skydiving and realize the sensation of free-falling is more relaxing for you than you realized it would be! Or perhaps there's an international cuisine you've never tried because you've always assume you will not like it. Perhaps it is time to try that Indian curry, or that pad Thai, or those dragon fruits you always eye at the market but never end up getting.

In short, you are never going to know what you find and do not find hygge until you actively try. You might even surprise yourself, so be ready to be open to all experiences!

When most people first implement hygge, they stick to what they know. But do not think for one second that hygge is simply about staying within those boundaries. Living a hygge lifestyle is also about branching out and pushing beyond your comfort zones to discover who you really are. The person who enjoys warm nights indoors on cold winter evenings might also enjoy bundling up and taking a crisp morning walk to watch the sunrise. But if they never do it, they will never know the extent to which their hygge lifestyle could expand. Therefore, experimentation and openness to new experiences can be fundamental to a hygge lifestyle. Give new things a try!

The "fundamentals" of living a hygge lifestyle are impossible to separate from how the person implementing it feels. It is all about how the concepts, starting points, and experiences trigger emotions and states of relaxation. The basics of a hygge lifestyle will always remain emotional. It is a lifestyle that is inherently shaped by the person living it, and no list of rules or commands will genuinely capture it. If an experience conjures negative emotions and a feeling of discomfort, it does not matter that the person next to them is enjoying it. To them, it will never be hygge. And that is fine. Hygge will always feel and mean different things to different people. Therefore, it is impossible to come up with a one-size-fits-all approach to the fundamentals of hygge.

All hygge fundamentals are truly individual, and it is—although potentially unsatisfying to hear—up to you to determine what the fundamentals of hygge are for you. As long as you're comfortable and giving yourself an adequate amount of winding down time and pleasure, then you're likely acting in line with a hygge way of life.

CHAPTER 3:

BENEFITS OF THE HYGGE LIFESTYLE

There are many different benefits to leading the type of lifestyle hygge offers. For many, reducing stress and all of the related health complications is paramount. However, for others, it will impact them in other ways, even though it still may offer more covert medical benefits. As with many different facets of hygge, the way the lifestyle will benefit an individual will vary. Although there are no specific benefits that all will share, some general benefits will apply to most people. So, let's get on to exploring precisely some of the benefits the hygge lifestyle can bring, and what you could do potentially to bring about those benefits.

The Danes—as well as other people from the Nordic regions—use a high-form of hygge that requires significant time spent outdoors, especially wandering through nature. Time in nature allows an individual to take in the natural beauty around them, unplug and get away from their electronics, and get the body and mind much-needed exercise by moving through and thriving in the space of a natural environment. Going outside and exercising is a healthy routine that will lead to a more satisfied, and more hygge, lifestyle. Many studies have shown that exercising outdoors, even with just a leisurely walk, can bring about more benefits than working out in a gym. If you can get up and get out, then do so, because it can bring about hygge and help you in times of need. It will get you in the right frame of mind for further hygge in your day.

Sometimes, when you are inside and trying to problem-solve, you can be too close to a problem, get frustrated, and not come up with a solution. However, if you get outside to change your surroundings and get your body moving, you will likely be able to develop solutions as you allow your subconscious mind to do some of the work you were trying too hard to assign to your conscious mind. Be sure to bring adequate water, food, and even a notepad when you go outdoors for an extended period of time. You can even bring your hygge comforts that lead to further benefits from engaging in this activity!

Hunting is another popular pastime in Danish culture. Being out in nature is synonymous with the clearing of one's head and leaving worries behind, as well as ensuring a meal is sourced in the wilderness and not merely bought in a market. Hunting engages and strengthens many different traits: composure, control, accuracy, patience, stillness, and respect for nature. However, hunting isn't for everyone, especially if you are a vegetarian or a vegan. In this case, you could perhaps learn how to forage and pick berries, fruits, and mushrooms. However, be sure you know exactly what you're doing when it comes to foraging—there are plenty of poisonous things out in nature!

If working hard and breaking a sweat in nature does not sound relaxing, simply being amidst it with only birdsong and a breeze passing through leaves to accompany you while you breathe in the outdoor air deeply can also be hygge-like. The outside air is crisper than it is inside your home, and, while it might be better filtered, pollution of the air in most homes is higher than it is outside. This means that "getting fresh air" can stimulate the brain in ways staying inside cannot, and this can be a real benefit that helps increase your levels of hygge.

Another significant benefit of hygge is what happens when stress levels in the body drop. Cortisol is the chemical usually associated with stress, but it has a broader impact on the body. It is a life-sustaining chemical that secretes from the adrenal gland and moderates a host of bodily functions. Blood sugar levels, metabolism, blood pressure, and immune responses are just a few of our bodies' vital components that cortisol influences directly. Cortisol naturally fluctuates as our body needs it to, regulating everything from blood vessel constriction to the leveling of sugars in the blood. With a fast-paced lifestyle, the body does not have a chance to return to a "normal state" before cortisol has to kick in and regulate something back down to normal.

These harmful cortisol levels can lead to a host of medical issues, which can worsen if the adrenal glands become fatigued because they can no longer keep up with the cortisol production necessary to regulate the bodily systems. This can result in sleep disruption, decreased bone density, blood sugar imbalances, and even reduced muscle mass. Not only that, but cortisol latches onto abdominal fats, securing them to their positions, which brings on a host of other medical issues. In essence, it is vital to regulate our cortisol levels by alleviating the stresses in our lives, something which a hygge way of living is excellent for.

Cortisol also contributes to the shortening of our telomeres, which ages our bodies faster. Telomeres are what protect our genetic information and sit at the end of our linear chromosomes. Have you ever thought about why world leaders seem to age so quickly when they take office? That's usually because of the high stress levels that affect their telomere lengths. Telomere reduction leads to aging skin and grey hair and affects an individual's lifespan. The more we control our cortisol through hygge-like techniques, the slower our telomeres will shorten as a result of stress.

From a biological standpoint, then, hygge is simply a moment where the reduction of stress and stressful outside influences improve overall health. Using hygge allows the body's cortisol levels to drop, allowing the body to regulate itself back to normal. If an individual indulges in hygge consistently, then the body has a chance to heal from some of the internal damage cortisol tends to inflict.

These couple of benefits alone increase the happiness someone experiences because the brain's chemical reactions are not being intruded upon by a constant surge of cortisol. Keep this in check, and work on how to release the brain's own feel-good chemicals like dopamine, serotonin, and oxytocin.

While there is a lot of emphasis on what is 'natural' within the Danish culture's interpretation of hygge, the simple fact is that the most significant benefit to this lifestyle is its lack of fundamental rules, as we explored in the previous chapter. Remember, being hygge is based on how you feel internally at any given moment, especially when you have unplugged from electronics, put away work, and found ways to unwind and de-stress. That being said, technology can also be used for hygge, especially if you love gaming, music, or film. It all depends on how you use it and the feeling that it invokes within you.

Therefore, the hygge lifestyle can be tailored to suit anyone. Some can find their hygge moments out at a club dancing in a crowd, while others will enjoy being alone and curled up on their sofa reading a good book. Both are hygge moments that can be found within wildly separate worlds simply based on how the person feels. The benefits an individual will get from these moments will determine whether their actions are hygge or not.

The lifestyle of hygge and what it promotes can also ward off certain mental illnesses. People who struggle with seasonal depression, drastic mood swings, and feelings of anxiousness have reported that making hygge their new way of life helps them regulate their symptoms. Through hygge, many have lowered their medication dosages, and a few have decided to come off their medications altogether. As hygge promotes a better lifestyle when it comes to individual health and focuses on being kinder to oneself, people often find they can deal with mental illness with newfound strength. This confidence can eliminate unnecessary feelings of guilt that can cause anxiety, halting an individual's negative carousel of thoughts. In this context, you could even call hygge a wonder-drug!

A fundamental fact of hygge is the absence of stress, but if you are in a stressful situation and cannot relieve yourself of it, hygge can then be utilized to deal with the stress more successfully. For example, you are already 10 minutes late for your workday, but you know you cannot give up that morning cup of coffee if you expect to be useful. So, when you drive to your favorite coffee shop, a hygge move could be spending $1.00 more to get a larger size and add your favorite flavor. You are likely to feel better about the extra indulgence, and you can relax knowing that you allowed yourself some additional comfort. Of course, this action might make you later, but it also might make you more productive. All you need to do is apologize for your lack of punctuality and even make light of it to coworkers. We're all late every now and then, and it's okay to slip up sometimes. At moments in which you think you've made a mistake, let yourself know it's okay to so you can move on. The hygge mindset will allow you to forgive yourself, as the feelings of guilt will otherwise get in the way of comfort. Remember, hygge can alleviate stress, so use it to help you calm down whenever you need to!

The benefits that come with a hygge lifestyle are not merely emotional; they are medical. Adopting the lifestyle that Danes consider a natural way of life has turned the lives of thousands of individuals around, and it is all because they decided to live outside of their own culture's norm. However, you may still not be quite sure how to apply hygge to your own life.

And for that, there is an answer.

CHAPTER 4:

APPLYING HYGGE TO YOUR LIFE

With hygge being such an interpersonal and reflective experience, outlining exactly how to apply its exacting aspects is near-impossible. I can give you examples and flesh out some scenarios, but remember the fundamental tenet of hygge: only the emotion it elicits from the person experiencing it gives hygge its meaning. Therefore, there is a lot you need to work out for yourself when it comes to applying hygge to your life. However, there are still tips and methods you can learn to help you along the way, and that's what this chapter is all about.

Many people who want to start implementing the hygge lifestyle say they feel rushed in their day-to-day life. The terms "stressed," "overworked," and "not enough time" frequently come up in conversation between people in Western countries like the US and the UK, and it is the pressure of this fast-paced lifestyle that makes them want a change in their lives.

At the very least, these people want to find a way to abate some of the stresses during their everyday lives. Western culture usually focuses on what's next, and many people find it difficult to wind down properly. Some take their work home, and some stay in their offices so late they only just have time to get home, eat dinner, sleep, and go straight back to work again. To apply hygge into your everyday life, you must spot the patterns of rushing around too much, trying to cram too many stressful things into one day, and give your body and mind the room to relax and unwind.

For many of us, vacations are full of hygge. On vacation, we tend to focus on relaxation, comfort, indulgence, and a slower pace. We also tend to surround ourselves with people whose company we enjoy. Maybe someone else has taken that vacation alone to experience the solitude life has to offer, in which case they are still relaxed, stress-free, and indulging in life's basic pleasures. For many, hygge is a simpler lifestyle, not because that quality is a requirement, but because modern life has become too hectic and complicated. Many of us are bombarded with constant alerts, notifications, and distractions. The lifestyle encouraged by hygge is one in which you implement the pleasures of vacations into your day-to-day life.

We might be used to electronics buzzing in our pockets or dinging on our dinner tables, but we are not relaxed around them. Those sounds quickly become associated with meetings, homework, angry bosses, last-minute assignments, and even domestic emergencies. These beeps and constant phone calls are not relaxing because our internal electrical signals have associated these sounds with emergencies and urgent messages. They cause a spike in our adrenaline, raise stress levels, and increase our heartrates. They work against what we seek to achieve with hygge!

Only when we relieve ourselves of these alerts and notifications can we begin to relax. There are many things we can do to achieve this peace and quiet. We can start by turning off our phones when we are outside of work hours. There's no need to allow everyone to contact you at all hours of the day and for you to always be available. You need that essential hygge time that'll allow you to unwind and enjoy life. Who wants to be twenty minutes through an engrossing movie only for someone to send you a work email that you could just as quickly answer the next day and not in the precious hours of an evening you're trying to enjoy?

The classical definition of psychological conditioning is a principle that makes hygge easier to implement. You may know this term from the behaviorist Ivan Pavlov's dogs with the bells experiment, where he conditioned dogs' mouths to salivate at the sound of bells because he would ring the bells whenever he brought them food. The result was that whenever he rang the bell, the dogs' mouths would start to salivate even without food.

We can use this conditioning on ourselves to get us to relax more and live the hygge lifestyle. You can condition yourself to feel hygge as much as your notification bells have likely conditioned you to feel anxiety or dread. Let's say you work from home, and your living room and your office happen to be the same room. You might, therefore, need to make changes to your room and condition yourself into relaxation. Once your workday ends, and you shut down your work computer, perhaps put a specific candle on, or change the lighting. These sensory signals can help you pair a smell or sight with relaxation, and you will be able to separate your workday from your at-home relaxation. Perhaps you could do the same by going outside for a walk as soon as your workday ends. You could even have a small reminder that pops up on your computer screen that it's time to get up and finish your day and go for a stroll. Or to play and follow a yoga video. Whatever it is that relaxes you and helps you find your hygge!

If you do not know what inherently relaxes you, then starting with a few basics can help. For example, try lying on your bed with the light on, and then turn it off. Did the light off make you feel panicked, even if a little bit? If so, darkness might not mean hygge for you. If you feel too exposed with the light on, then maybe the light is not hygge for you. If neither the light on nor off elicited any sort of response, then experiment with different types of lights. Try a group of lit candles or a machine that casts colorful patterns on the ceiling. Try using lightbulbs for which you can change the color with a remote. Try adhering glow-in-the-dark stickers to something in your room. Experimentation is your friend here. Sometimes it isn't the lighting, but the room that promotes a specific feeling, so you could even try the experiment in another room. Hygge goes further than an emotional experience. It is a creative experience, and you can find novel ways to shift your environments to produce a hygge-like experience within you.

Pay attention to how your body reacts to things like lighting, smells, the temperature of the room, coziness and comfort, music, and anything else you can think of. The more you pay attention to engaging your senses in the best possible way, the closer you will get to discovering your inner hygge. And don't feel bad if you don't work it out right away; you will get there in time. There's no need to rush—be hygge about it!

For some, slipping into hygge gradually is necessary. Drastic and significant changes make some people anxious, and that defeats the point of hygge. If you are someone who struggles with rapid change, then be sure to implement new techniques more slowly so you can get used to it. The point of applying hygge to your life is to abate and dwindle those adverse and emotional knee-jerk reactions to things to bring about more bliss and other positive emotions. So, try a few simple things at a time: keep your favorite candy at your desk at work, or purchase a travel coffee mug with your favorite color or design on it to hold your coffee in the mornings. If you are someone who enjoys colorful or mismatched socks, consider wearing them underneath your clothes. Even though others might not see them, you will know they are there, and they might make you smile. The point with these types of deliberate implementation of hygge-like actions is that they can all contribute to the overall purpose and experience of hygge.

A smaller gesture is taking two more minutes in the bathroom to sit and breathe in the stall. Maybe you are not ready to implement colorful coffee mugs and mismatched socks that make you smile. Perhaps you long for a couple of minutes to yourself where someone is not trying to get in touch with you. If that is the case, then use your bathroom breaks at work or home to accomplish this. Slip into the bathroom, leave your phone behind, and sit for a more extended period of time. Take in deep breaths through your nose and close your eyes. Relish the fact that no one is calling your name, and you do not have to answer to anyone but yourself.

But perhaps you want a bit of social interaction at work. If your work has a kitchen, then maybe go there and make some coffee or tea and talk to anyone else that is doing the same thing. Perhaps you could even offer hot drinks to others around you. You'll be doing something nice for people, and you'll get to be in the kitchen longer than you would have anticipated originally!

Sometimes these types of hygge-like moments are all someone needs to abate their stress hormones and push them back down to a healthier level. Anything that will help you relax, be it at home, in the car, or at work, will bring about more of a hygge mindset. When facing stress or decisions, perhaps ask yourself, "What is the most hygge-like thing I can do right now?" And you'll likely start making decisions that will help you be more relaxed and satisfied in the future.

Many people also wonder about hygge-style foods. Foods that are considered "comfort-inducing" are, almost always, synonymous with "unhealthy" and "fattening." People wonder if that type of thing can lead to an unhealthy lifestyle that eventually brings the opposite of what they want to experience.

Hygge is not a lifestyle of overindulgence. Just as never relieving stress is toxic for the body, overindulging brings about a different type of toxicity. In this regard, the hygge lifestyle, when it comes to food, can be described as "a break." Living a healthy lifestyle and making sure your body is taken care of is of utmost importance. However, allowing yourself a double-scooped ice cream cone every now and again may be right for you. If you turn your back on everyday pleasures all the time, you likely do not have a hygge-like relationship with food and yourself. Give yourself a break. If you follow the hygge lifestyle adequately, it will not lead to unhealthy habits; it is the lack of self-control that leads to a lifestyle to no longer be hygge-like.

Food has a more prominent role to play than mere consumption and its associated benefits. You may find that cooking, baking, and plating up a satisfying meal rewarding. Some may consider measuring and controlling the exact ingredients in recipes relaxing and comforting. In contrast, many others may feel the act of eating half of the cake batter before it even hits the pan hygge. Some people enjoy putting the food on a plate in an aesthetically pleasing manner, and even more people enjoy cooking meals and then taking them to someone else to enjoy. The hygge possibilities with food are endless, so do not stop at the mere consumption of it. If you haven't learned to cook yet, but you've always wanted to, then why not start now? You can try cooking simpler foods like pesto pasta or any other simple favorites you might have. If you're exceedingly confident, perhaps you could even share your meals with others. Your possibilities with food really are endless, and you can start finding out what flavors go well together, what spices go well with what vegetables, and which wine complements a specific cheese!

If you wonder if there is a specific percentage of hygge that has to be found each day for you to be living a hygge lifestyle, you run the risk of having a Dane chuckle at you. A complicated emotional feeling goes way beyond any attempt to take something and boil it down to statistical analysis. No, hygge isn't something you can measure or see on a pie chart because it's way more individual than that. You can fill your day with as little or as much hygge as you desire, and it is up to you how satisfied you feel with the outcome.

However, for those who do not feel self-aware enough or do not enjoy experiencing deep and potentially intense swells of emotion, hygge is hard to implement and understand. For Danes, hygge is something that they practice every day. From the chimney sweepers to the mayors of their biggest cities, hygge is a regular part of the well-being of the person experiencing it.

And the fact that it spans social classes and people from all walks of life might make hygge seem mind-boggling. But rest assured, it is a straightforward wide-ranging philosophy and way of living.

Applying hygge to one's life is like starting any new habit: at first, it has to be intentional, and it will likely feel foreign. Sometimes it has to go on calendars or in someone's phone reminders, and sometimes people even have to write it on a sheet of paper and pin it to their refrigerator or above their desk. Either way, the constant reminder will be helpful to making hygge second nature. Although many people would think this defeats the purpose of hygge, in a society that runs on the ingrained impulse of "constant" activity, scheduling "downtime" is almost necessary to make it happen. In other words, intentionality and planning can help you live a hygge lifestyle and not be detrimental to it.

Like any habit, hygge will work its way into the daily routine of the person implementing it, and if it holds any sway or value in their lives, they will make time for it. Even though some days might make hygge more challenging to implement, having a few methods to keep the lifestyle a priority will be more useful than implanting no hygge principles one day and loads of hygge principles the next. Like keeping in touch with a best friend or checking up on a beloved neighbor, hygge will become more of a habit the more you work it into a daily routine, and it will end up becoming something to look forward to rather than a difficult challenge to overcome. The more you focus your mind on creating hygge experiences and cultivating precisely what that looks like and means to you, the more quickly it will become second nature. You won't even have to think about it, and you will essentially become an honorary Dane!

Therefore, the true application of hygge is when it becomes second nature. Remember to practice it daily and as much as possible, and your present and future self will reap the constant rewards and benefits.

However, one rule that is synonymous with hygge is "unplugging." Turning off your phone, shutting down your laptop, and getting off those videoconference calls is imperative to the application of hygge. Sure, it might seem odd for a concept that is supposed to have no definite rules, but there is a physical and medical benefit behind switching off. Therefore, you should probably pay attention to it.

When we spend too long staring at screens, it is unlikely that we are doing so in a good posture or breathing correctly to give our lungs and bodies the vital energy needed for optimal output in any given day. When we breathe correctly and allow our minds to wander, we will likely be happier and more creative. We are all too quick to fill any downtime or any moment of potential boredom—like when one person goes to the bathroom in a restaurant, and the other person instantly takes out their phone—to fully take in the world around us. One word of advice is to turn your phone off at certain times of the day. Perhaps you're at home, and it's after 9 PM, or you're out to a restaurant with a friend or loved one. These are good times to turn your phone off or put on silent and place out of reach. Don't worry, your phone isn't going anywhere. So, unplug in the knowledge that you can look at your social media feeds later!

There are many theories about whether or not the EMF

(electromagnetic frequency) signals emitted by our daily bombardment of electronics negatively affect our bodies. However, these theories haven't entirely passed the speculative stage. On the other hand, there have been many conclusive studies performed on what our obsession with technology has done to us and how staring at screens negatively affects our sleep, as we shall discuss.

Our eyes have photoreceptors that prompt the waking up and shutting down of our bodies, and they affect the release of melatonin—a hormone in the pineal gland that tells our bodies that it's time to sleep. Because of these sensitive photoreceptors, it is essential to switch off the lights and electronics early if you want to fall asleep at a suitable time to wake up on time. Our photoreceptors help align our natural circadian rhythms (the inward and natural clock our body runs on) with the outside world. When these signals are activated, specific responses are provoked, and those responses prompt either alertness or sleep to overtake the body.

So, when someone is up and on their phone at 11 PM or watching television in their beds at 1 AM, the light glaring from their electronics will interfere with their regular sleeping patterns. The blue light emitted from these devices blocks the release of melatonin, making it far more difficult to fall asleep. Coupled with this, you should associate your be with sleep and not any other activity. If you are looking at your phone with your back pressed against your mattress, reading a newsfeed, thinking about politics, or any other topic that is likely to induce stress, you will start associating your bed with that type of stress. This stress is not conducive to sleep. For starters, you should set up time earlier in your day to look at these types of things (if at all), and you should also put "worry time" into your schedule.

You might chuckle at the term "worry time," but bear with me—it is a fundamental concept to help you sleep better. When we spend our days switched on, we give our minds little or no time to wonder. By the time we lie down in bed, all the worries and concerns we blocked out using technology throughout the day will surface when we lie down to sleep. If we deal with these concerns earlier, sound sleep will likely come. And sound sleep is hygge—you do not feel your best if you are sleep deprived.

But what are some of the dangers that sleep deprivation can bring?

Sleep deprivation can lead to a host of negative things such as a higher risk for strokes, memory problems, a greater chance of traffic accidents, and even hallucinations. Here is a good lesson Westerners can learn from the Danes—when we sit in our chairs, we do not need to spend hours staring at our phones. Alongside its disruptiveness to our sleep patterns, our harmful postures (we even have the term "text neck" to refer to the lowering of our heads when we stare at our phones too much) also negatively impacts our eyes because we have to strain them when looking at all the small text coming from a bright light. When you disrupt your body's natural circadian rhythm, it will wreak havoc on your sleeping patterns and compromise your health. In short: staring at your phone impacts your life for the worse, and it is also shortening it.

Be more mindful of your technology consumption because overindulgence is nowhere near the ballpark of what hygge means.

If there is any one way to sum up the implementation of hygge accurately, it is this: turn it off, lay it down, and breathe slowly, deeply, mindfully, and through your nose. There is an inherently slow pace to a hygge moment or lifestyle simply because of the fast pace our society seems intent on keeping. From moments that create fond memories to lying in the dark and just existing, you can find hygge in the simplest of places as long it reduces your stress, anxiety, and panic. Getting away from the constant dopamine hits of buzzing and ringing technology is an excellent way to calm your body and mind and relax your way into a hygge state of being.

The hygge lifestyle is rooted in medical reality and psychological principles that form our physical and mental health foundations. Hygge brings to the forefront a self-awareness that serves the medical needs we must understand for the rest of our lives if we are going to live life to the fullest.

Hygge is not a fad, or a trend, or something that will eventually fade into the background. Instead, it is a way of life that promotes good health benefits on a physical, emotional, chemical, and hormonal level. Remember this, and you will find it easier and easier to apply hygge to your life—no matter what the season is.

CHAPTER 5:

HOW HYGGE DIFFERS WITH THE SEASONS

Despite the stereotypical pictures of cabins covered in snow and other images used to represent hygge and its lifestyle in the heart of winter, hygge transcends seasons. As the lifestyle can be tailored to a specific person depending on their emotional and physical state, seasonal changes only serve to promote more hygge-like moments, not diminish them. The changing seasons encourage creativity in finding hygge-like moments even when the environment changes. The typical pic-

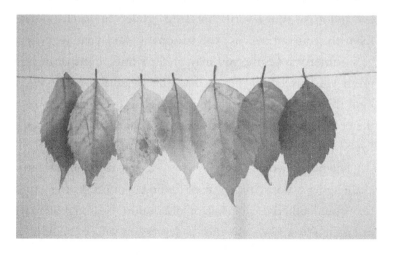

tures we tend to see of fuzzy socks, steaming hot cups of spiced apple cider, and groups of flickering candles are all beautiful things, but that is because the lifestyle of hygge is concentrated mainly within just one culture on the planet. So, we are most familiar with how Danish hygge-like moments have manifested in the types of climates and curiosities their country has to offer. However, there are ways to integrate it into your culture.

So, now we know that hygge is not seasonal, although the seasons will affect your implementation of hygge. If you are someone who enjoys long walks on the beach and feeling the sun beat down on your face, it does not mean that having a hygge lifestyle is only possible during the summer. Beaches are open all year long, and in many places in the world, the sun still shines in the winter. If the sun has been gone a few days, consider traveling to a place where the sun is shining, or perhaps even indulge in a low-light tanning session. If you are someone who enjoys knee-high socks, large blankets, and hot mugs of apple cider, then your hygge is not only possible in the wintertime. You could sit outside at dawn, or crank the air conditioning, or sit in the basement, dress warmly, bundle up under a throw blanket, and make your favorite hot drink while you watch a movie. Even so, you can still use the seasons to find your own hygge in other ways. Sure, you may prefer winter, but that doesn't mean you have to spend all the other seasons longing for it. Find things you enjoy in the heat as well as things you enjoy in the cold. Doing so will maximize your chances of experiencing hygge year-round!

For many people, hygge is a way to get through the more challenging seasons. It is a way of finding comfort during a time that could otherwise be full of discomfort. Seasonal affective disorder, also known as seasonal depression, affects millions of people every season, from summer to winter and back again. However, it typically comes on during the winter months of the year due to the lack of sunlight. Sunlight is responsible for giving our bodies vitamin D, and when it is weak, tucked behind the clouds, and cold out, we are not going to get enough of it. Many of us do not think to take vitamin D supplements because we do not realize that vitamin D plays a major role in balancing chemicals throughout the brain. When your brain is starved for something that makes it stable, it becomes unstable. This instability can lead to difficult symptoms such as fatigue, depression, brain fog, and malnutrition. A lack of vitamin D can wreak havoc on the body's metabolism, disabling it from drawing the nutrients out of the food it needs in order for the body to function properly. People report decreased appetites with low vitamin D levels, sluggish behavior, stiff and aching joints, and even chronic headaches.

These types of symptoms are why part of the hygge lifestyle focuses on nutrition. Ensuring you get what nutrients you need, no matter the time of year, means your body and mind will be kept fully functioning. This type of bodily care is essential to one's mental state, which holds a great deal of influence over the physical body's responses. If the mind is suffering from a chemical imbalance that results in depression, a lack of appetite can create issues such as malnutrition, dehydration, and muscular tissue degeneration. If the depression is causing someone to eat constantly, then the rapid weight gain can result in a higher risk for strokes, heart conditions, bone fractures, and osteoporosis.

The importance of the body's physical health is paramount. Therefore, you should utilize the nutritional supplements available to you and introduce hygge into your world, which can help quell the debilitating issues that surface due to seasonal affective disorders. The more you spend time seeking the comfort hygge can offer you, the less likely you are to suffer from mental, emotional, and physical ailments due to seasonal changes. For many, supplementing the lack of vitamin D and eating healthy during the autumn and winter months helps with their seasonal depression. For those who experience it in the spring and summer, attending to things such as allergies and getting tested for allergic reactions, various pollens may help you understand why seasons affect you the way they do.

Furthermore, winter might make it difficult to exercise because it may be too cold outside. Therefore, it might be a good idea to find exercises you can do indoors, be it yoga, workout videos, or your own routines that you make up. Exercising releases necessary endorphins and hormones that will help keep you in high spirits through any season, but especially in winter!

However, know that seasonal affective disorder is different for every person, and utilizing some of these methods does not mean it will dissipate fully. For some, seasonal affective disorder is merely about coping with a season they do not enjoy. If someone does not like the snow or the hot summer months because the temperature of the environment or traveling conditions are not ideal, they can become stressed. This induction of stress can wreak havoc on the body and someone's ability to function with their job, family, and friends. Therefore, not only does it affect the individual, it can cause people who live with or around the sufferer a great deal of hardship.

For the above reason alone, the implementation of hygge throughout all seasons is imperative because it can combat some of these issues that many of us face year-round.

As discussed, winter is the season when most people suffer from low moods. Keeping the body at a comfortable temperature while it is cold outside is ideal for reducing the amount of stress the body is under. Therefore, using heaters, fires, wearing extra layers, warm socks, drinking hot drinks, and having hot showers and baths can all contribute to the experience of hygge. However, these are not the only things considered hygge during those winter months. Watching a movie with a friend, staying in bed longer during a day off from work, and sitting still and breathing mindfully are also considered hygge. They help relieve stress and will give the body a chance to repair itself from the stress of a day-to-day routine.

Other activities that can help in the winter months are extended conversations with a good friend, belly laughter over jokes, and watching a great movie in your favorite pair of pajamas. Remember, you do not just have to implement hygge in a social context; it merely has to serve its purpose of de-stressing you. Alone or in a group, you can always find moments to implement more of it.

In the spring months, hygge can come in a variety of forms. Many people enjoy walking through fields of freshly bloomed flowers, and many enjoy going on leisurely nature walks through their neighborhoods after the cold winter months melt into memory. Many enjoy being able to bring out shorts, dresses, and other loose-fitting clothing, and others find peace sitting on their porches and watching the wind blow through the spring trees as they inhale the sweet scent of grass. Spring is a time for growth, and this can be a necessary mindset when it comes to ensuring that your spring is full of hygge and hygge-like moments.

However, some people struggle with seasonal allergies during times of bloom, so inhaling a bunch of pollen and plant dander may not be ideal. These allergies may cause some people to stay inside more of the days and to shut their windows from the outside air, which others would deem fresh. Even so, it is still possible to be hygge in the springtime. For one, going to see a doctor and getting some answers and medications for your allergies can be hygge in and of itself because not only can it provide solutions, it can give relief from allergic reactions allowing a sufferer to more fully enjoy all that spring has to offer. Even long showers to wash off that irritating pollen can be hygge, as can going on a drive through the countryside rather than a walk. Many wooded areas and mountainous terrain trails have alternate routes for cars, and the views are spectacular. You can take the drive with friends to create memories or drive alone to secure some peaceful time for yourself. Either way, drive carefully and be mindful of your surroundings to give yourself the best possible hygge experience!

No matter what you decide to do in the springtime, it is hygge as long as you care for your health, reduce your anxiety levels, and treat yourself to something that makes you smile.

Hygge in the summer months is what many people look forward to. For many, beach trips, long and barefoot walks over the sand, swimming in lakes, hiking through a forest, and even tanning are just a few of the ways the summer months can bring about relaxation and hygge. Many enjoy wide-brimmed hats, sitting out in the sun, and drinking an ice-cold beverage. Others enjoy the familial activities that tend to come with the summer months, like picnics and backyard barbecues. However, some people do not have close relationships with their families or do not enjoy the beach, which is perfectly okay. There are other things summer can provide that will give you the full hygge experience.

For example, if you do not enjoy the heat, swimming pools might fit your fancy when it comes to unwinding and relaxing.

Maybe lounging around the house in grungy shorts, a baggy t-shirt, and pouring an ice-cold drink is more your style. Perhaps you do not enjoy the beach at all but do enjoy the dizzying heights of the mountains. Going to the mountains during the summer can be perfect for two reasons: 1) the mountains are always a few degrees cooler because of their higher elevation, and 2) the colors of the trees, flowers, and greenery are in full bloom. It makes for beautiful pictures and a serene environment packed with the sounds of nature, wild animals, and a lovely summer breeze. Make sure you keep your distance from the wild animals, though, and never feed them. It is essential not to meddle in nature's affairs as you marvel at it.

In the mountains, like most places, you have options. You can take friends or family, or you can go by yourself. Whichever sounds more comforting and rids you of the anxieties of everyday life will always be the preferred method when leading a hygge lifestyle. You can hike to get some much-needed exercise or drive through the open countryside to enjoy the majestic views. Either way, it is up to you what you do in the mountains. You can even go to a campground and stay for a night or a weekend. You can then fully experience the mountains and unplug from your everyday life.

Finally, we can think about hygge in autumn (fall). Especially in the US, autumn brings about holidays like Halloween and Thanksgiving and even Oktoberfest events inspired by Germany. There are so many things that make people smile and jump for joy during this season: hot apple ciders, pumpkin pies, familial celebrations around tables of food, and the leaves changing into all sorts of exotic colors. Hot temperatures begin to subside into 70-degree days. A cool breeze rustles the leaves in the trees, and the weather becomes temperate enough for anyone to enjoy a nature walk or an outdoor theater production. Many things can be considered hygge during the fall season, from long sweaters and luscious boots to comfortable sweatpants and delicious desserts. Not to mention the pumpkin-spiced lattes that your local coffee shop is likely to sell! Many enjoy spending time with their families, while others prefer to sit on their porch and watch the leaves slowly change colors. Many people love lighting their seasonal candles scented with autumnal spices and turning off the lights in their home, and many others enjoy lying in the dark with their windows open as the smells of the outside autumn waft in.

No matter the season, there are always opportunities for hygge. Many find their joys within the seasons, from seasonal meals and desserts to temperatures fit for bundling up or going for a walk. Sometimes it may reflect who the individual shares the season with and what the promise of a specific season means to them. Winters denote snuggling and cuddling up to those you love while watching beautiful movies, and autumn reminds people of delectable treats they will consume as they approach the holidays. Spring boasts new life and new adventures for a new year, while summer means vacation times, sun-soaked laughter, and exploration. All of this can be enjoyed with friends, family, or alone. Just remember, there is a difference between choosing to be alone and feeling lonely. The former can bring about a wonderful experience of hygge. The latter can ruin the hygge experience if it promotes sadness and negative emotions.

Again, hygge is a deep-seated feeling that transcends seasons. It wraps up those stereotypical ideas of seasons into an ongoing lifestyle. No longer are these scenes and images things to just aspire to, but the hygge philosophy can allow you to re-categorize them into a fulfilling way of life. You do not need to just dream of the next season each time you are in a season you like less. Find ways to enjoy every season, and you will discover your hygge each and every day, elevating your levels of comfort, happiness, and fulfillment.

When you fuse hygge with the seasons, it not only brings about relief and a different way of life, it also brings about hope. The hope is that the images we associate with the seasons become true-to-life experiences available to anyone, no matter what.

And sometimes, hope is all we need.

CHAPTER 6:

HYGGE ON A BUDGET

With all of the beautiful things mentioned about hygge-like moments throughout the seasons, many also need to keep things within their budget. As previously mentioned, hygge transcends social classes. Therefore, it is more than possible to implement hygge without spending a ton of money. Today's "millennials" have been proven to be the first generation that will not only make less money than their parents throughout the course of their lifetime, but they will have a lower standard of living than their parents. They will be the first generation to not progress beyond what their parents achieved, although they will establish their lifestyles differently. For example, millennials travel more, change jobs more often, and take more time off than the generations before them. And, with the high-octane culture many of these millennials live in, they will need stress relief tactics above and beyond what they are familiar with on a regular, daily basis.

The modern world's economic realities also mean today's young people need to keep hygge within a specific budget. But that is okay because you can implement hygge without spending an additional penny. Remember, turning off your phone, sitting still, and breathing is hygge. So, hygge can be free, but let's explore some of your low-cost hygge possibilities.

Many millennials cannot afford the gas money to take those luxurious mountain drives or indulge in a beachfront rental property vacation. Many more cannot afford the ingredients to cook lavish meals or purchase those $42.00 quote-inscribed candles in all their various scents. For many, merely indulging in a bath bomb is a step outside of their budget.

So, how can you create a stress-free lifestyle within the limitations of a budget?

For starters, if you are a candle lover, many websites sell off-brand candles and other candles that are not entirely up to manufacturer quality. Think of them as the "Dollar Store" of the retail world, but in candle form. You can find many rare scented candles that have inscriptions on them on websites for $5-$10, and even more websites will give discounts when you purchase a certain number of candles. Likewise, various smaller towns have legitimate candle factories, where employees create homemade candles in the back and then sell them out front. Buying candles from these types of places lowers prices drastically because they cut out the middleman. You can even purchase battery-powered electronic candles that can last far longer than a wax candle ever could. Sure, you won't get the same scent or heat emitting from them, but you will still benefit from the lighting.

When it comes to food, plenty of people do not have the budget to purchase their favorite pastry from their favorite market. But there's a way around this. Why not buy the ingredients on your own and make your own pastry? If you do not like baking, then perhaps work that pastry into your already-set grocery budget. Maybe you can dispense with that unhealthy pack of sodas or opt for cheaper toilet paper to free up some funds for your favorite pastry, all while not going over your shopping budget. Your hygge-goals have options here. Be creative!

Another way to reduce stress and find hygge-like moments that do not cost anything is to go out for a walk. Rather than getting in your car and using gas, which is detrimental to your wallet and the environment, just leave your house and stroll around your block. Consider putting headphones in but be extra careful when blocking out sounds around you—you will not hear cars in the street, people, or animals. Even if the scenery around your block isn't the most exciting, merely moving your body while listening to your all-time favorite playlist can elicit positive emotions, which have significant benefits for the overall reduction of stress as well as balancing brain chemistry. I also challenge you to find the beauty in your scenery, as beauty is everywhere. Try listing your ten favorite things about walking around your block to ensure a positive experience!

Another way to do hygge on a budget is to find a way to make your favorite coffeehouse drink. Many people spend up to $80 a month at a coffeehouse when they could spend half of that and make twice as many drinks at home. However, I understand that some people utilize their favorite coffeehouse as an excuse to get out and around people—and the experience in a coffeehouse can be hygge in itself. If that is the case, purchase small packages of your favorite flavored creamer and use them when you buy a standard coffee from your favorite coffeehouse. You'll save money in the long run and still enjoy those hygge-inducing flavors!

Another way you can do hygge on a budget is to consider creating your own entertainment. You don't need to spend money going out for a movie. There are so many streaming websites out there, although many of us do not realize just how much it costs us to have them all running. If we use too many sites, we could be racking up huge bills over the year and not really notice how much we really spend as costs of streaming from multiple sources come out of our accounts often, on different days, and in smaller bill amounts. You can also go on your computer and find entertaining videos and films on YouTube, which you do not have to pay anything for. For those looking for alternative entertainment, consider checking out your local library. You can pick out a good book, take it home, curl up on your couch, and immerse yourself in another world and it will not cost you a penny (as long as you do not bring the copy back late!). You could even get an audiobook from your library if you prefer listening to stories rather than reading them. You may even find a quiet nook in a library full of colorful nature magazines and decide that is hygge in itself. If any of this sounds like you, get yourself a library card and begin reaping the benefits of this free entertainment.

If it is too difficult to get to a library, or the cost of getting there is too expensive, you can still create hygge in your home. You can create your own nook! Dig out old blankets, find a comfy chair (or, if your budget allows, purchase a cheap bean bag chair). Stuff it with used books or anything else in your home that you consider hygge. Light the nook to perfection with candles you already have, or perhaps use a soft lamp. If you have to buy anything, perhaps scour the internet for daily deals and slowly piece something together without ever going beyond your financial means. Again, if you need to, make room in your budget by giving up something else so that you never spend beyond your means. Alternatively, you can go to thrift stores, flea markets, and rummage sales to find spectacular deals. People tend to sell used or unwanted items for a bargain—they're often trying to get rid of them more than they are trying to make a profit! Take advantage of this market to create your own nook, and before long, you can sit in your own little slice of hygge heaven.

If you decide that you need to spend a bit of money, you can find many proverbial gems at low prices. Everything from books to candleholders to antique bookshelves is sold at way below their traditional value at thrift stores. Therefore, it is easy to walk in with a small amount of cash and walk out with all the tools and items necessary to put together your dream relaxation nook. Be sure to remember mood lighting! You can use candles or twinkling fairy lights but make your space as comforting and personalized as possible, so you have the freedom to unwind. Express yourself! Paint your fantasies into it! Remember that finding hygge is all for you and all about you.

Thrift stores are not just useful for creating your own nook; you can create your own comfortable wardrobe from them. If you need new clothes and do not have money to spend on lavish items, these stores are plentiful. Many people find their most comfortable pieces of clothing hanging on the racks in thrift stores, from old knit sweaters to marked down fuzzy socks. You can find everything from handmade blankets to fleece-lined comforters, and even those who enjoy collecting coffee mugs or beer glasses will find themselves immersed in a world that their hygge thrives in. And, just like the library, many people find browsing thrift stores hygge in and of itself. Looking at all the weird and wonderful things in these stores can be enjoyable, as can trying on fun clothes you'd never opt to buy. Therefore, do not rob yourself of the joy (and incredible bargains) a thrift store might bring you. Remember, hygge is not merely about just being comfortable; it is about finding new things and ways that make you cozy. It will comfortably expand your horizons. Take advantage of that.

To benefit from another form of hygge, you could make yourself a simple, slow-cooked meal. And, before you worry about how much a chuck roast, carrots, celery, and onions cost, understand that a slow-cooked meal does not necessarily mean an expensive meal. If you purchase a package of chicken breasts and some Alfredo sauce, you can simmer that in a crockpot on low heat for six hours, boil some noodles, and have yourself an Italian feast! If Mexican cuisine is what you fancy, buy chicken breasts, dump in a jar of your favorite salsa, and cook on high for four hours. Maybe you don't like to eat meat, and you want to slow cook yourself a delicious mac 'n' cheese. Then so be it! A slow-cooked meal does not have to be expensive to make you salivate and sink into the couch while the smell wafts over you from your kitchen. A warm meal in your stomach is relaxation enough for many people, and there are several two-ingredient crockpot recipes out there that will satiate anyone. You can even cook a large amount of this meal, portion it out, and freeze whatever leftovers you have. You will then have meals for days and will therefore be able to relax in the evenings when you do not feel like cooking and cannot justify spending money on takeout.

Although a spa is relaxing to many, the cost can put it beyond a hygge budget. However, that does not mean a spa day is out of reach. Giving yourself a self-care spa day at home is simple, fun, and can be done for a relatively low price. You can purchase your favorite nail polish color and apply it yourself. Or you can use gentle hand soap and a bowl filled with warm water to soak your feet and hands in to scrub off all that dead skin. You can use bath bombs, bath salts, and skin-softening bath bubbles that will make you hum with joy. You can buy cheaper face masks, body creams, and hair masks. Better yet, you can just buy coconut oil and give your hair a deep condition. Just because you cannot afford the $300 price tag for a salon spa day doesn't mean the relaxation of a spa is out of the question! And the money you spend on a do-it-yourself spa day is a wise investment because many of the items will last longer than a single day so that you can have multiple spa days. You could incorporate these spa days into your weekly routine and have many of them. That extra bit of self-care will keep you happy and in the hygge mindset as much as possible.

It's even possible to consider therapy as hygge. We all have issues we need to discuss in one way or another. Sometimes, the best path to healing ourselves is to speak about our lives openly. Talking to a professional who offers insight when necessary may offer a more objective view of your life, which is relaxing to some. However, many therapy sessions are not covered by insurance, and many others cannot afford the insurance that does. You could then consider talking to a friend of a family member. Although talking with a friend who knows you well can prove to be even more stressful than not talking at all, it is often beneficial. If you are the more introverted type and want to benefit from a form of therapy, consider keeping a journal to externalize your thoughts. If you do not like to write with a pen, then open up a document on your laptop or desktop computer. Keep a journal (whether it's paper or electronic) to help get your thoughts out and in order. Although there might not be anyone listening, you will still be expressing your vital thoughts and emotions without judgment or ridicule. Sometimes it can be cathartic to know that your thoughts, emotions, and judgments have been unloaded somewhere and are no longer cooped up within you. Write it down, and let it go!

Also, to use a bit of self-therapy, you don't need to write diary entries or into your journal. You could write poetry, stories, or draw pictures if that's what you find relaxing and hygge-inducing. There are no right or wrong answers here, just whatever suits you best! And don't be afraid to try a combination of things. Just because you are talking with your friend about your problems doesn't mean you shouldn't also write a journal. In fact, keeping a journal will likely help you remember the issues you need to deal with and can provide a framework for you to bring up your issue with a friend in the first place.

If you are still paying for a video streaming service, then you don't need to worry about spending any additional money to find your favorite movie there. Having the steaming service and using it will always be cheaper than going to the theater, too, especially for how often you are likely to use the streaming service. Furthermore, indulging in a bit of nostalgia by watching an old film you love can conjure positive emotions that compound positivity in the body. Movies that elicit laughter and happiness cause the brain to secrete dopamine and serotonin, two of the main chemicals in the brain associated with happiness. These neurotransmitters also help preserve lifelong brain function, abate seasonal depression, and help you sleep better. So, if all you have is a streaming service, throw on a comedy or a feel-good movie that you love and get lost in it! It will leave you with more lasting effects than just making you smile in the moment.

A few people find gardening relaxing, but many people who would otherwise enjoy it are deterred by the idea of digging massive amounts of dirt while the sun is high in the sky. This is the exact reason why people invented indoor gardens. You can employ tactics from a cheap hydroponic garden all the way to potted plants that thrive without sunlight that will go easy on your pocketbook. Several people have installed kitchen sink gardens and grow anything from fresh herbs and spices all the way to their own pineapple plants from right inside their homes! Better yet, you can start many of these plants by using scraps from the foods you already purchase at the store. Simply buy the pot and soil, and you are ready to create your very own peaceful indoor garden—without the mess of a traditional garden!

Living a hygge lifestyle does not require much money. All it requires is a yearning desire to be stress-free, even if you only achieve this in spurts. Always remember that hygge is a feeling and not a concept. Concepts have rules, and sometimes those rules become expensive, like fancy diets that come with their own measuring tools. With hygge, you simply need to treat yourself kindly and remember to breathe. These two ideas side-by-side create the perfect habitat for the physical, mental, and emotional health to thrive. The hygge lifestyle lets you be creative and find activities that come at no cost to keep you relaxed throughout your day. So do not fret if you feel the pressure to spend money because that's what you think hygge is. Hygge is for everyone, everywhere, regardless of personal or financial circumstances.

You do not have to live your life in a constant state of stress-induced anxiety and exhaustion. You do not have to sacrifice yourself for your job continuously. It is possible to work hard and still find time to relax and focus on yourself.

And that is what hygge is all about: focusing on yourself.

CHAPTER 7:

HYGGE AS NEW EXPERIENCES AND CULTIVATING MEMORY

W hen you think of hygge, you may think of it in terms of comfort of the present moment. Although this idea is somewhat correct, hygge can also be about forming new memories by going on adventures and trying things you've always wanted to try but never given yourself the time to do so. Therefore, hygge is not exclusively about relaxing. You could find hygge in thrill-seeking moments, or in those special times that you hang out with your families. If you act in a way you know will create new, novel, and exciting memories for you, your life will be more enriched as a result. With this newfound enrichment, you will form memories that you can use as a form of hygge and comfort during your day-to-day life as you lie on your sofa, wind down after a difficult day, and retreat into nostalgia.

Although you might feel comfort in following the same routine over and over again, and you may even find this somewhat hygge in itself, you also run the risk of stagnating and becoming bored or frustrated—the antithesis of hygge. Therefore, the richness of a new experience could fulfill all your hygge needs, and the memories these experiences can form could contribute more strongly to a fulfilled life than if you were to play it safe by not stepping out from your comfort zone.

Therefore, the formation of new memories is absolutely essential to hygge. The only way you will recall old information and compare experience is through memory, and your memory will help guide you to experiences you deem to be hygge. If you cannot remember how hygge feels due to the lack of experience you've had with it, how will you draw from your knowledge in order to seek it? If you only use a lavender candle every time you wind down at the end of the day, how do you know you don't also like citrus candles? How do you know that you don't like citrus candles even more?

The answer is you won't know unless you try it. Therefore, hygge is a process of experimentation and an openness to new experiences, whether your experiences be large-scale and lifechanging like traveling to a region of the world that you've never visited before to summit a mountain, or whether the experience is as simple as adding a different flavored syrup to your morning coffee. New sensory and bodily experiences can open up a new world of hygge you may never have known you enjoyed otherwise. And perhaps you find out that you do not like something new that you tried. Fine! Then you know not to do it again. You only know what you've learned.

Psychologically, the human mind forms memories easier when it experiences significant moments. Many trivial events happen to us in our day-to-day experiences, and most of that triviality gets lost once the present moment passes. However, memories have a way of keeping a record of the past in their own unique way. Memories can be notoriously bad for recording specific details. Therefore, even if memories feel clear to an individual, there are many aspects that the brain will "imagine," filling in the gaps their memory has failed to fill itself. However, the mind tends to be good at recalling overall experiences.

Think about it. If you try to remember something that happened every hour of every day over the last week, chances are you will forget large chunks of time because nothing significant happened. However, if on your way home you tripped over your shoelace and dropped your coffee on the ground, and shared a laugh with a passerby, you'll have that in your mind and a funny story to tell at a later date. Your mind may forget exactly what you were wearing that day, omit the exact coffee you ordered, or the color of the eyes of the passerby—but you will remember the most crucial part of it clearly. If you see the funny side in this situation, you it will likely be more of a hygge-like experience when you consult your memories. Making light of otherwise embarrassing situations can lead you to feel calmer and even make you chuckle!

To apply how we form memories for hygge, consider engaging in different activities that you find new or exciting that will more likely lead to the creation of positive memories. You can also think of how we tend to do this on specific days throughout the year. People will always ask you what you did on Christmas, and the chances are you will remember because the holiday is significant. What other days is a family together, eating a delicious meal, and handing each other gifts? Not many, if any at all. Therefore, when you try to cultivate hygge in the form of a good memory, enrich your experience by testing new or novel things.

Have you always wanted to go rock climbing? Then give it a go. Not only might you enjoy the experience in itself, but you will also be able to form a positive memory that you can think back to if you keep going back and getting good at it. The same goes for cases in which you've always wanted to take up a sport, or you've always wanted to go to a national park, and you keep promising yourself you'll go, but you keep making excuses as to why you shouldn't. Once you do these things, you can determine whether you found them hygge or not. If you do, then great! You can rinse and repeat. If you do not, then no worries! You don't have to do it again. When you apply your hygge mindset to new experiences, you will increase your chances of having experiences that will lead to excellent memories that you can hold on to for the rest of your life.

Remember that, over time, memories can fade. A good way of keeping these memories alive is by writing down your experiences—which strengthens them internally and keeps a record of them externally—or taking pictures of things you do. Use these supplemental methods to assist your memory and increase your hygge experiences. Furthermore, perhaps you go on a walk every day, and you take the same route every day. Try a different route, write down how you feel about it, and maybe take some pictures of cool wildlife or a tree that makes you smile. The world around you is alive and electric. Even if you live in a city, walk down roads you have never been down before, and give your mind something new to consider. But make sure when you walk down unfamiliar streets that they are safe!

Perhaps you want to form memories, but you need to do it in the comfort of your own home. Then maybe try and do things inside that you've always wanted to do and never had the motivation to. Want to build your own shelf? Then give it a go. Want to write a letter of gratitude to a friend? Then sit and do that. When you do these things that are novel and new, not only will you enjoy them, but you will also have a new memory to show for it. And memories are fundamentally essential to us as human beings. Not only do they give us stories to share and enrich our experience when socializing with others, but they also allow us a positive sense of nostalgia when reflecting back on an exciting time in our lives. When we age, our activity levels dwindle gradually. When we have more novel memories, we can create feelings of hygge in our own heads when our bodies become less capable. Therefore, the hygge way of mixing new experiences with memories is by thinking long-term!

To truly reap the rewards of hygge memory, though, we need to ensure we have the correct perspective in everything we do. Remember that hygge is not related to material things, but to how we view the world around us and take actions based on those views.

CHAPTER 8:

HYGGE AS PERSPECTIVE

While some may experience hygge as a feeling, a philosophy, or even a fad, the fact is that hygge is a perspective. It is a way of viewing all aspects of life, from day-to-day activities to life-defining hopes and dreams. Every aspect of life will take on a hygge perspective when you begin to live a hygge lifestyle. Understanding the true nature of hygge is critical for anyone who wants to incorporate it into their way of life.

Without this understanding, hygge can go the way that countless other traditions and cultural movements such as hippies, Bohemians, and hipsters have gone: into oblivion. These traditions started as a lifestyle revolution, promoting a different approach to life, love, and happiness. They all had a direct impact for a while, affecting how people lived in a great many ways. Unfortunately, as time progressed, these movements' true nature got lost in the hype of commercialism, which replaced the hippie's outlook on life with overpriced hippie-style jeans, blouses, and even incense. Likewise, the Bohemian movement's lifestyle became little more than a fashion trend, with some musical genres incorporating the name. This cycle of events is seemingly inescapable since materialism's overwhelming influence seems to always corrupt, co-opt, and assimilate any other culture or way of life it comes into contact with. No matter how powerful a movement is when it begins, eventually, it succumbs to the relentless influences of the consumerist culture surrounding it. In other words, it goes from counterculture into mainstream culture, with the latter especially corruptible by materialism. That said, if you want to incorporate true hygge into your life, it is imperative that you keep hygge safe from the cultural assimilation that has befallen countless popular modern movements. The key is never to lose sight of the fact that hygge is a perspective and that no commercial interest or influence will ever corrupt that.

One way to keep the true nature of hygge as perspective alive and well is to continually distance the concept of hygge from the things that help manifest it. A perfect example of this is the use of candles to create a hygge environment. While it is true that candles, and the light they provide, can create a feeling of hygge in any room, referring to the candles themselves as hygge misses the point. Candles are candles, nothing more and nothing less. The experience you have with the candles could be hygge, though. Therefore, a candle branded 'hygge' would be incorrect as the material has no inherent meaning. It is your perspective that makes them hygge or not. And, as we discussed earlier, hygge comes down to your interpretation. Nothing can promise to satisfy your unique outlook on hygge.

Unfortunately, many people will begin to call candles hygge, thus starting the cycle of turning a way of life into an advertising campaign. The more we call various objects hygge, the stronger the corrupting influence will be. Such is the course of a capitalist market.

This corruption is precisely what happened to the Zen tradition. While Zen took on a unique form in Western culture—becoming something akin to hygge—it was usurped by consumerism. Now when you discuss Zen in the Western World, the first thing that another person may envision is Zen candles, Zen water fountains, or even Zen tea. In other words, rather than imagining the core feeling and mindset of Zen, many will conjure up images of the product line sold at their local market. You can undoubtedly create a Zen environment or even a Zen mindset by burning candles, listening to a water fountain, and even drinking hot tea. However, you can also create a Zen mindset by taking a walk in nature, spending time with one of your loving pets, or listening to soothing music. Sadly, the items used to achieve Zen goals have become mistaken for the goal itself. Any person who is genuinely interested in Zen and in attaining a Zen mindset will steer clear of the objects that have the name "Zen" attached to them, as they know that this is nothing more than a marketing gimmick. Buying into these products perpetuates the falsehood that Zen can be purchased in a store, and the nature of being Zen can be reduced to something that has monetary value. Fortunately, enough people are aware of the problem and are striving to return the true meaning of Zen back to its original definition. Zen, like hygge, doesn't require that you spend any more money.

But hygge faces the same challenge that Zen has faced, and still faces, in Western culture. Before long, candles will be given the moniker "hygge," as will blankets, slippers, mugs, and even varieties of hot chocolate. In fact, it will probably only be a few more Christmas seasons before you will be able to purchase a hygge gift set, complete with all of these things in a "genuine" Danish gift basket. Therefore, it is imperative that anyone who engages in the practice of hygge maintains the true meaning of the concept and upholds the individualistic, personal and anti-commercial nature of this fine tradition. Never allow yourself to buy things just because they are attributed to the hygge lifestyle—you should only buy something if it helps provide you with a genuine hygge experience. Certainly, candles help establish hygge because they allow you to turn off electric lights and unplug from modern technology. However, this doesn't mean that you need candles to be hygge, or that a candlelit room is necessarily hygge.

Let's use a metaphor. Think of hygge as getting yourself into shape. Sure, you can buy things that help you get into better shape, like weights or spinach. However, merely buying these things won't get you into better shape. You can get into shape by using them or eating them. However, you can also get into shape without buying weights or spinach. In that way, for hygge, you can buy tools or supplementary materials to help you achieve a hygge mindset, like candles. Still, candles are not absolutely essential for you to accomplish a hygge state of mind.

The most important thing is determining what hygge means to you and deciding what items are necessary to establish it in your heart and mind. After all, that is the whole point of hygge—it is the process of creating a specific state of mind. It is your perspective. It doesn't discriminate based on the seasons. This state of mind can be defined as cozy, joyful, peaceful, or any other positive word that best describes what hygge means to you. Just as hygge can mean many different things, it can also take many different things to manifest it. You should be sure not to get caught up in the 'tools of the trade.' You can find hygge despite the tools that could get you there. Keep your mind focused on the feeling of hygge and the impact that the feeling has on your life.

Another essential aspect of hygge is that it can only be understood when—and if—you consider hygge as a perspective. That aspect is that hygge comes from within, not from without. As such, the key isn't to try to find something that possesses hygge in order to create the hygge experience. Instead, the trick is to find things that *inspire* the hygge that already exists in your heart and mind.

As a state of mind, hygge is something that has to be aroused, not ingested. This state of mind is why people can find hygge in a wide array of objects and experiences. The objects and experiences don't contain hygge; instead, the individual using them possesses a hygge state of mind. Subsequently, you take hygge with you wherever you go and whatever you do. Knowing this will help keep the true meaning of hygge alive and well in your mind, and it will help you encourage others to stay on the right path towards their hygge, too!

Instead of using things traditionally associated with hygge, begin to explore all of the things that resonate with the hygge that resides within you. There will be many things that you will consider hygge—one of the most enjoyable aspects of it can be finding exactly what you determine it to be. You might be surprised at the things that can inspire a hygge response within you. They may be things associated with your childhood, or they may be things related to your favorite color, fragrance, or even flavor. Sure, hot chocolate is commonly referred to as an integral part of hygge, but if chocolate isn't your thing, it's important for you to find something else that works better. It is vital that you don't simply follow what others are doing, as this is another road to turning a lifestyle into a trendy cookie-cutter trap. Instead, use what others do as a point of inspiration. Start with hot chocolate, for example, but move on to other hot beverages that you might like, such as tea, lattes, or even hot mochas. Or you might not even like hot drinks, so you can merely try drinking orange juice instead. There is no need to latch on to the fad just for the sake of it. However, you might find that someone else uses similar tools as those you use to experience hygge. And that is fine! Even in our individual interests, there will be some overlap. Use the hygge-interests of others as inspiration for your own.

Something else to consider is the fact that hygge isn't a fixed point in time. Just because something inspires hygge one day does not mean it will have the same effect on another day. As a result, it is essential to discover various things that inspire hygge so that you can alternate among them, as your mood requires. Your perspective is absolutely crucial here. A perfect example of this is reading. For many, reading can ooze hygge. However, there might be a time when your eyes are tired, or your body isn't in the mood to sit for an extended period of time. In these cases, reading, no matter how hygge it might usually be, may not induce that feeling. Remember that you can also "read" a book using an audiobook!

Remember, hygge is flexible. Instead of reading, a walk in the woods, a bicycle ride, or any other more physical activity might suit your body's needs at that moment. Alternatively, if your eyes need a rest, then simply listening to some soothing music while you relax with your eyes closed might just do the trick. Since your mood and energy levels will change from day to day, it is vital to remain flexible with your hygge practices. By recognizing that hygge comes from within, you will depend less on specific activities to nurture your hygge state of mind. This will enable you to choose from a wide variety of things, meaning that you can access different tools to suit your different moods and energy levels.

This flexible approach to hygge can take on a seasonal connotation, especially in countries with a broader range of seasonal climates than Denmark has. In parts of the United States, where it can get extremely cold in the winter and extremely hot and sunny in the summer, tapping into different sources for hygge can be extremely beneficial. While sitting by a fire might be just do the trick in the dead of winter; relaxing on a beach, listening to the sounds of the ocean, and feeling the gentle summer breeze might do the trick in the heart of summer. Discovering your various faces of hygge will help keep you maintain a hygge state of mind all year long, regardless of the season or the weather conditions. Like everything else, the only thing that really changes is your perspective. Therefore, it is vital that you remember that your hygge is within, waiting to be "switched on," and external stimuli can help you achieve this goal. This knowledge will help keep you from getting stuck in a rut with certain hygge activities. Sure, fireplaces and hot chocolate are fantastic, but you can't rely on them in July in Florida! (And this is where the flexibility comes in—try having a delicious ice-cold drink instead.)

Therefore, by finding what inspires your hygge in every likely scenario and environment, you can rest assured that your hygge will always be within reach. Finding hygge inspiration in many things also means that you won't have to pack an extra suitcase to bring your hygge items with you when you travel. The less reliant you become on specific objects, the more likely it is that you will be able to experience hygge no matter where you are. This holds true for business trips as well as vacations. If you have to travel for business, you must find numerous and simple ways to nurture your hygge mind. It can be as simple as bringing a candle with you to the hotel, bringing a home comfort like a pillow (or even a stuffed animal!), or comfortable slippers you can wear about the room. Even business trips do not have to make hygge difficult. All you need to do is hold on to the notion that you bring your hygge with you, no matter where you go. Again, perspective is fundamental!

While it is true that you shouldn't get too caught up in specific items or activities for maintaining your hygge mind, it is also true that when you find something that works, you should use it fully. If you fall in love with a particular piece of clothing, such as a sweatshirt, and it fills you with hygge each time you wear it, then wear it as often as you can. Don't be afraid of what others might think or say. Wear your sweatshirt every day if you want, because it matters how you feel and what will give you the experience of hygge. In the case of summer clothes, maybe you have a favorite pair of sandals or a favorite t-shirt that arouses your inner hygge every time you wear it. If you want to wear socks with your sandals down to the beach, so be it! It's up to you to love what you wear, and not for other people to decide. Use it as long as it works but know that you can find other things to take its place if it stops working. Stay flexible, pay attention to your body and mind, and maximize your hygge perspective as much as possible.

Music can also affect your perspective and inspire you into hygge. Sometimes you will come across a song that just resonates completely, overflowing your hygge levels like a river in a rainstorm. You might be tempted to play the song repeatedly, listening to the music and lyrics until you feel as though you could burst with the hygge you feel. Eventually, you might wear the song out by listening to it too much, or you might find something else to take its place; however, as long as it does the job, you should listen to it as often as you can. The important thing is to keep your hygge alive and well at all times. Therefore, whenever you discover something that achieves that goal, use it as much as you possibly can, no matter how boring or annoying it might be to some people around you!

CHAPTER 9:

HYGGE AS A CREATIVE OUTLET

You can apply hygge to your creative life and use its mindset to improve how you live in various ways. Creativity can give you an abundance of mind-healing properties and meaning. Having a creative hygge mindset can enrich your experiences as you become more in tune with your inner self and your external surroundings, and you will be happier regardless of your internal or external circumstances. One of the best ways to have a healthy mind is to express yourself creatively. Just like hygge itself, creative expression manifests in various ways and can mean different things to different people. Some may find cooking an elaborate meal or baking a delicious homemade treat to be a profoundly creative act. Some may find hygge in the more traditional artistic outputs—painting, sewing, writing poetry, singing, taking pictures and editing them, making homemade videos, and even dream journaling. You may even find it creative to make that nook in your house that we discussed earlier!

One of the main benefits you can get from engaging in a creative activity to foster a hygge state of mind is that you can use your individuality to express yourself in an authentic and calming way. You can express the strength of who you are most effectively if you apply the principles of hygge to every "brushstroke" of your creative efforts.

You can find comfort even from your darkest thoughts if they manifest tangibly in front of you, no matter whether you are writing or taking photographs. Perhaps you've always wanted to take up a creative hobby and, up until now, you've made an excuse for yourself like "I'm always too busy" or "I'm always too tired." Well, when you apply hygge, you will find more energy. You can make creativity a habit and use it to foster hygge.

There's a difference between the traditional work-oriented mindset plaguing those who live in the US and that of other Western societies. Often, an American feels too busy to engage in what they perceive as "play." They usually center their focus around their work and jobs, to the detriment of meaningful creative expression.

Creativity is fundamental to a healthy mind. Although it can be playful, it goes well beyond this narrow definition (in a way similar to the fact that hygge goes well beyond mere comfort). Therefore, in order to foster a hygge mindset creatively, it is essential to free up some time on your calendar and start using your mind and body to create something special and meaningful for you. It is in this freeing up and boundless potential for creativity that makes hygge possible for any individual.

To direct your energy onto something creative will help you maximize your enjoyment of life and potentially provide you with an abundance of hygge. Creativity can be relaxing, help alleviate stress, and help individuals make peace with their environment. Too often, we can feel stuck indoors and bored with nothing to do. We scroll endlessly through newsfeeds on our phones, and buy things we don't need to try and fill the meaning-shaped hole burning inside us. There may be days that you want social interaction, but all of your friends and family are busy. Therefore, there's nothing quite like creating art and indulging yourself in these quieter moments of solitude and self-reflection.

Your options for what you consider hygge are endless. You can make art, enjoy it yourself, or take pictures of it and share it with your friends and family. Hey, it might even be hygge for you to write a poem or paint a piece of art, and then let it go by throwing it on a fire—whatever is most hygge for you! If you share it with friends and family, and they, too, are dedicated to the hygge mindset, they may even take up a creative activity themselves. This attitude will provide you with a chance to explore yourself individually when it comes to a creative expression of hygge and spread the good vibes to others around you!

Have you ever walked around an art gallery, read an incredible book, or watched a brilliant film, and wished you could create something beautiful yourself? The best news is that you can, even if you've never engaged in the hobby before. Look at any actor, poet, artist, or singer. They all had to start somewhere, and when they began to express themselves, it wasn't the fantastic stuff we all get to experience today. We all have to start somewhere and accept that we are the well-to-do fool on the quest for mastery. In short: there's no shame in being a beginner.

The sheer act of creation comes with a multitude of benefits. By writing stories or journaling, we can make sense of our lives through narrative, as humans are naturally narrative driven. We can laugh, cry, release, and express through this form of creativity uniquely. It is a way to externalize our minds even if there is not a single person around to experience it with us. But if there are other people around, we can share our stories with others. Consider how great it is when others share stories with you. Consider how much you love telling stories yourself. They are a way for us to bond and come together over the dinner table with family or in a café sipping coffee with a friend.

If you're too self-conscious about your artistic output or feel low on energy, you can engage in less taxing forms of self-expression. For example, you could start a collage. Take magazines you love, images off the internet, or words and phrases from a newspaper you have. Cut them up and stick them on a board that best reflects what hygge means to you. You can find positive words from the newspaper and pictures of people smiling in the sun or the snow. It all depends on what fosters hygge within you. Perhaps hygge means a variety of things to you that are distinct from one another. Maybe you love summer and winter equally. Perhaps you could create two different collages, one for summer and one for winter. Or maybe you could do a collage where you dedicate half of it to winter and the other half of it to summer. The contrast could even be beautifully hygge itself! You could incorporate your own thoughts and feelings in the collage by creatively cutting out words from various headlines and making them say what you want them to say.

You could even engage in the creative process with the word "hygge" specifically in your mind, or you could even write it on a sticky note and put it in front of you as a constant reminder to your conscious and subconscious mind. Perhaps you can write a poem that features the word hygge. You could make rhymes about precisely what it means to you and the positive impact it could potentially have in your world. Before you get creative, you could even make your favorite drink, have a glass of wine, or eat a square of dark chocolate—whatever is most hygge for you! You could sit in the nook you may have already made in your home, or you could go out into nature and draw under a tree, or sit and write a poem in your favorite café. The possibilities really are endless.

To think about the present mindedness that poetry can bring to the hygge mindset, envision the Japanese poetry of haiku. Haiku is a three-line poem under 17 syllables. It often reflects one moment in nature and captures it in the form of a written snapshot. Haiku writers will look at the natural world and convert it into a satisfying moment of beauty, seeing simplicity (although, if you ask a haikuist, you will realize how complicated it really is). Haiku helps the mind be more hygge. It encourages the writer to interpret the natural world more regularly and pay attention to the present moment rather than rushing around to do the next thing on the never-ending to-do list.

If you decide to do something like writing a story or a poem, or you start taking stunning pictures and editing them, you can share them with others. Perhaps in your city, there are poetry open mic nights. Perhaps there are local galleries you could share your photos in. You could even hang pictures you make and poems you write in your home to remind you of hygge at all possible moments in the day.

If you're an extrovert, you could even have social art sessions. You could all sit with friends and do a writing prompt and share the results with each other after, or you could sit with your friends, sip delicious wine, and focus on creating art. You can even regress back to the days of childhood and finger paint! Anything that encourages a hygge state of mind works here.

If you are struggling and unsure of what to do about creativity, perhaps you can start a dream journal. A dream journal is basically as it sounds—a journal where you log your dreams. As soon as you wake up, record your dreams in the present tense, as if the dream were happening right in front of you. Doing this is essential for a variety of reasons. First, you will recall your dreams more easily and see connecting themes throughout different dreams you have. The positive aspect to this is that your dreams' healing capabilities will improve and your subconscious interaction with your conscious brain will be more robust. Having the subconscious and the conscious brain work symbiotically can lead to greater satisfaction, let you focus your energy where you really need to in life, and will help you develop a balanced hygge state of mind.

The problem with some of Western society and why so many of us are unhappy is that we are a consumerist culture rather than a culture of creation. If we spent less time-consuming other people's work, and more time producing our own, we would benefit from a hygge state of mind more often, and we would be more satisfied. If you're lucky and fully creatively engaged and motivated by that energetic spark, perhaps you could even experience a "flow-state" as a result of your creative expression. This state, coined by psychologist Mihaly Csikszentmihalyi, a cofounder of positive psychology, is "The best moments (that) usually occur if a person's body or mind is stretched to its limits in a voluntary effort to accomplish something difficult and worthwhile." Therefore, if you engage in a creative practice, you are placing a necessary demand for your intellectual faculties. Although hygge is about a state of pleasure and relaxation, you can experience both of these when expressing yourself with a paintbrush, pen, or camera.

The most important way to merge hygge and creativity is to realize the stress-relieving and happiness-inducing effects of it. Externalizing what goes on in your brain is exceptionally hygge as it leads to an overall sense of wellbeing. When you sit down to be creative, perhaps put on your favorite music, or even just the sounds of a waterfall or chirping birds to get you into that mindset. Make the area you are creative in as comfortable and hygge-like as possible. Perhaps put blankets and pillows on the floor before you start writing something, throw on some sweatpants instead of those uncomfortable jeans, light some candles, or use an aromatic diffuser to delight your senses as you delve deep into your inner self.

Creativity and hygge go hand in hand. You can decorate your house, paint, write, take pictures, sing, and find so many ways to express yourself. There's a reason why so many people choose to express themselves even though the process can sometimes be a little complicated. We may even hit creative "block," which is better to think of as a creative "hurdle"—a challenge to jump over, not be stopped by. Indulge in the marriage between your conscious and subconscious mind and take up a hygge-like creative endeavor whenever the feeling and mood suits you!

And with that, we can move into what hygge can do for you more broadly and how you can apply it to all aspects of your day-to-day life.

CHAPTER 10:

HOW TO BRING HYGGE INTO EVERYTHING

t's easy to find advice and tips on discovering or creating an environment that provides and nurtures a strong sense of hygge. From turning a cozy corner in a room into a hygge shrine or nook to locating that perfect place in nature that oozes hygge, establishing a space for all your hygge needs is essential. Some will call this space their "happy place." Others will just call it relaxing. Whatever you decide to call it, the point is that you should feel hygge in everything that you do. Once you realize that hygge is a perspective, you will understand that you can find it in just about any environment. While I highly recommend creating a sacred space or finding a perfect sanctuary in order to restore your hygge, it is not the only way to practice hygge in your day-to-day life. Instead, the trick is to practice hygge in even the unlikeliest of places. When you are able to restore and nurture your hygge no matter where you are, and no matter what you are doing, you will be well on your way to creating and benefitting from the hygge lifestyle. Implementing hygge no matter the situation is a critical difference between someone who dabbles in hygge and someone who adopts hygge as their way of life. The art of practicing hygge anywhere and at any time might be difficult at first, but once you get the hang of it, it will soon become second nature to you. And it is because of this second nature that you will genuinely benefit from all that hygge has to offer.

Some of the environments where you can practice hygge might not be ones you would expect to find on a list of recommendations. That is because a lot of times, when you think or read about hygge, you encounter hygge stereotypes. Therefore, it's best to look at examples of where you can practice hygge and get the most out of your new lifestyle and mindset. One such example is the grocery store. Depending on your personality, going to the grocery store might be a fun thing to do, or it might fill you to the core with dread. From having to deal with crowds of people to spending more money than you ever wanted to, grocery shopping can be a challenge even for the most easygoing people. How you react to this experience can determine how well you cope with the stress of it. Herein lies the true nature of hygge. Rather than wishing yourself away from the moment, longing to be in your quiet and cozy home far away from the hustle and bustle, utilize some of the hygge techniques you've been learning in this book into your grocery shopping experience. How you do this is up to you, but one option is to bring some earbuds and play some hygge music to drown out the stressful environment around you. Another trick is to treat yourself to something that restores your hygge state of mind. Fortunately, many grocery stores have incorporated coffee shops, making this practice easier than it would have been not so long ago. Rather than running through the grocery store at full speed in order to get out as soon as possible, take a moment to buy a cup of coffee, maybe even a pastry, and casually roam through the aisles as you indulge in something that brings you to a state of hygge. By taking things easier, you can get your grocery shopping done without stressing yourself out in the process. Furthermore, by establishing this routine, you will stop dreading your visits to the grocery store. In fact, you might even start looking forward to them, and appreciate the hygge benefits they can offer!

Another example of turning an unpleasant situation into a hygge experience is when you are stuck in traffic. Driving back and forth to work every day can be stressful enough without any added hassles. Unfortunately, those added hassles will too often find their way into your commute. Sitting in traffic and hearing the proverbial clock tick second by second can be enough to drive anybody crazy—especially if you're already late.

The thing about scenarios like these is that they are beyond our control. Not only are they unpredictable, but they are also utterly unchangeable once you find yourself in them. Rather than letting such circumstances create untold levels of stress and anxiety, take the opportunity to restore your hygge with the added time you suddenly have. One way to make sitting in traffic better is to play some music that helps to restore your spirits. If you run the risk of being stuck in traffic from time to time, make sure that you have special CDs, music tapes, playlists, or even books on tape specifically designed for those occasions. By creating a playlist to get you through that situation, you can turn any traffic delay into a hygge experience, thereby restoring your energies and relieving stress. You can even decide to do a bit of learning by listening to an audiobook or a podcast. Heck, you could try and do a guided breathing meditation as you slowly move through traffic. Doing so will lower your heart rate and cortisol, making your trip relaxing, enjoyable, and hygge. Now, instead of getting to your destination tired and frustrated, you can arrive rested with a smile on your face and a skip in your step. Engaging in activities like the listed examples will ensure that circumstances do not determine your mood, and this will help cultivate your hygge mindset at all times.

The workplace is yet another environment that can cause all sorts of stress and anxiety if you do not treat it with the all-important hygge mindset. This is especially true for anyone who works in an office setting where the décor is drab and boring at best and downright depressing and claustrophobic at worst. Cubicles, gray carpets, beige walls, and fluorescent lights can drain the energy from anyone, no matter how cheerful their disposition might be. The trick is to make sure that you have the opportunity to unplug from the dull, drab surroundings and immerse yourself in some healthy hygge energy. Pictures and objects that inspire hygge can go a long way in turning any lifeless workplace into a hygge environment. Unfortunately, not everyone has the option of decorating their workplace. Therefore, they need to employ other methods of maintaining hygge at work. One alternative method is to make use of aromatherapy. While you might not be able to burn incense or light a candle, you can still utilize fragrant scents in order to evoke a strong sense of hygge. Placing a dab of essential oil just over your upper lip will enable you to breathe your favorite fragrance all day long, with the added benefit of not bothering anyone else. You can keep several different bottles of oil on your desk or in your drawer so that you can keep the scent strong all day long. Additionally, you can change scents during the day to suit your mood. Just be sure to use essential oils that are gentle on the skin and that can wash off easily with just warm water.

You can also try things like bringing hand creams and lip balms with you to work. That way, you can take care of your skin while you sit at your desk, increasing the amount of hygge you're likely to feel at work. Keeping your skin healthy will keep you relaxed and help get you through the day in the calmest and best mood possible for the circumstances!

As mentioned earlier, music can go a long way to establishing a positive hygge mood. Some workplaces will allow you to listen to music as you work, in which case you can create your hygge environment quite easily on a regular basis. However, in the case that you cannot listen to music while you work, make sure that you bring some tunes with you anyway because you can plug your favorite music in while you eat lunch or take a coffee break. This can make all the difference in the world, helping to transport you to your happy place, thereby restoring your mind to a full sense of hygge before tackling the rest of the workday.

When you combine the use of music with the use of essential oils, you will engage two of your five physical senses, meaning that nearly half of your senses will be devoted to creating and maintaining a hygge state of mind. If you can also have visual aids, such as pictures or objects on your desk or screen savers, you can take time to focus three of your five senses on achieving hygge. When you can devote most of your physical senses to hygge, you will achieve more substantial results in no time.

Another thing you can do while you're at work is to use your lunch break to do something that's more hygge-oriented. If you bring your own lunch to work, then you don't need to worry about getting out and finding lunch, which will save you both time and money. Perhaps, then, you can go for a walk outside and sit on a bench and eat your lunch in nature. Or maybe it's too cold outside, but your office has long hallways. Then maybe you could do a bit of exercise to keep your mind alive. You can walk the hallways as mentioned above, or even the stairs, to get in a little bit of exercise. Not only will this keep you healthier, but it will recharge your brain by flooding it with natural and healthy chemicals so you'll be ready to tackle the second half of your workday.

The effect of using objects to achieve a hygge mindset should not be underestimated. In fact, the use of objects to induce a chosen state of mind is practiced worldwide in many different forms. A prime example of using objects is in the context of religion. Millions of people worldwide, including religious people, use objects and symbols daily to evoke a sacred mindset or remind them of their particular faith. These objects can come in many different shapes and sizes. Sometimes they will be large and prominent whereas other times they will be small and discrete. No matter the event or circumstance, the impact that these objects can have is often beyond measure. Fortunately, the very same dynamic can be achieved with regard to hygge. The fact of the matter is that particular objects and symbols can evoke a strong sense of hygge within a person, much like a cross or a Buddha-figure can evoke spiritual feelings within a Christian or Buddhist, respectively. That said, it is absolutely critical that you discover what objects or symbols have this effect on you. As mentioned earlier, placing objects on your desk at work can profoundly impact your creation of a hygge environment at your workplace. However, when that option isn't available, you can try to incorporate smaller objects, such as jewelry, to achieve the same goal. You can pick something sentimental to you or something that makes you feel more positive and puts you in a go-getter mood. You could even wear a locket that has a picture of loved ones inside it. There's no right or wrong choice here. It only matters that whatever you choose inspires hygge in you!

When you wear a bracelet, ring, or even a watch that holds a particular hygge significance, you can evoke a hygge mindset each time you look at it. The trick is to find several such accessories or pieces of jewelry that have a hygge feel to them so that you can surround yourself with them as often as possible. Additionally, having numerous pieces of hygge jewelry or accessories will mean you have a hygge object to accompany formal wear, casual wear, and everything in between. The benefit, then, is that you can be hygge no matter what type of clothing the day calls for. Again, keep in mind that hygge means something different to different people. Therefore, the trick is to find what objects create a sense of hygge for you. Cat charms, pendants, or earrings can have this effect, especially if they remind you of being at home in your cozy chair with your cat in your lap. Alternatively, natural stone bracelets or pendants might remind you of your favorite place in nature, which can also evoke a hygge mindset. You might wear a watch or a piece of jewelry from your favorite museum or another place you go that helps you restore your spirit after spending time in the bustling world and restore your hygge energy.

Clothing is also a potentially powerful tool for creating hygge energy. As mentioned previously, certain comfortable clothes can help establish a sense of hygge when you are at home. However, you might not want to opt for these clothes outside of the home—and you may be completely unable to wear them if you are at work. No matter how hygge they can feel, you just can't show up to work in your favorite pajamas! But just because you can't wear your comfortable pants or sweatshirt to work doesn't mean you can't find clothes that inspire hygge. In addition to comfort, color is another way that clothes can foster hygge. Different colors inspire different moods in people, so it is vital that you take the time to find out which colors inspire a sense of hygge in you. Colors associated with winter might remind you of cozy environments, which could create a hygge mindset whenever you wear them. Or you might choose earth tones to remind you of your favorite nature retreat. The mere act of wearing your favorite color might help you complete that task at work, and you might even sense a glow from your co-workers. Maybe the clothing you wear will even inspire a feeling of hygge in them. In the end, no particular color is necessarily hygge in and of itself. Instead, a particular color should represent a hygge place or a hygge experience in you. Take the time to find colors that restore your hygge energy and make sure to fill your closet with them. This awareness and action will enable you to bring a little hygge with you everywhere you go.

So, our day-to-day actions and choices can affect our experience of hygge. It doesn't matter where you are, what you're going to do, or what type of clothing you need to wear, hygge truly can be brought into everything. You can bring it to your home, workplace, car, school, family gatherings, park, bar, theater, and anywhere else you might go. The essential lesson from hygge is that you can enjoy pretty much anything if you bring a hygge mindset to it. Whenever you next feel stressed, or you're dreading going into work or getting in that car, just remind yourself that you always have hygge. Once you recognize that you have it with you at all times, your life will improve drastically.

Now that you've learned how to bring hygge into everything, let's move forward and see how hygge manifests itself in Western culture.

CHAPTER 11:

SIGNS OF HYGGE IN WESTERN CULTURE

A lthough hygge is a Scandinavian word that cannot be easily translated into English, it does not mean the concept itself is alien to Westerners. Just because the English language does not have a single word that epitomizes the idea of hygge does not mean that it is not prevalent throughout Western culture. However, when you begin to truly understand the concept of hygge—which you are well on your way to doing so as a result of how much of this book you have already read—you will realize that these seemingly isolated phenomena are actually different elements of hygge emerging within Western culture. That said, it's no wonder that so many people are becoming interested in a hygge-like philosophy, no matter what they are calling it, as the seeds for it have already begun to take root under different names. Once you connect the dots of these different forms, you will begin to get a clearer idea of the essence of hygge from a Western perspective. It is not critically important that a single word cannot encapsulate hygge. What is essential is that the spirit of hygge is fully understood. Only then can hygge be implemented to its full potential within the life of an individual and within Western society as a whole.

One of the earliest forms of hygge that's prevalent in Western culture is tea consumption in England. For the past couple of centuries, drinking tea has been the cure-all for almost any trauma or circumstance imaginable. Just as a cup of coffee has become necessary for many to start the day in the USA, the proverbial English "cuppa" has become the go-to for dealing with any stressful situation. Tea-drinking is a perfect example of hygge in Western culture. In order to fully appreciate the similarities, it is essential to understand better how drinking tea becomes a part of someone's life in England and much of Great Britain. Initially, a person is introduced to tea at a young age, usually drinking a milky version of the beverage prepared and served by their mother (due to its caffeine content). This can sometimes evolve into the "tea party" game in which a child pretends to serve tea to their guests, usually comprised of several stuffed animals of various shapes and sizes. Tea drinking is a ritual of comfort and is used on any occasion. And this is where drinking tea begins to acquire its hygge status. After all, the mere act of drinking tea could become enough to take a person back to the innocent and safe days of their childhood. Just a sip could conjure up memories of a mother or father brewing them some delicious tea. Even if not, when an English person goes to someone else's house, one of the first things they will likely be offered is a cup of this hot beverage. It's no wonder that tea is the first thing that many people go for when trying to cope with a stressful situation. Nothing else can restore a sense of comfort and safety for a British person quite like a good cup of tea.

Perhaps the example of tea explains why the word "cozy"— although it goes part of the way in explaining hygge—does not fully capture hygge. If an English person had to choose a single word to describe the feeling that a cup of tea provides, cozy will likely not be at the top of the list. However, it is still an act of hygge! But words like "homey," "safe," "peaceful," and even "comfort" might come to mind, but even then, no two people will necessarily agree on which word works best, as we all should know by now. The fact is that a cup of tea evokes feelings that no single word can express fully, but there's an emotion there all the same.

Furthermore, a cup of tea can evoke different feelings in different people. Therefore, rather than trying to find that single word that expresses the true meaning of hygge, we should stick to finding examples of hygge that Westerners are already familiar with. Thus, when trying to describe hygge to someone in England, you can say that it is like drinking a cup of tea, and they will instantly understand the essence of hygge, which, after all, is far more important than the word itself.

Another form of hygge that can already be found in Western culture is the concept of "comfort food." In essence, this concept follows the tradition of hygge in two ways. First, it reflects the use of the term hygge as a root word, forming words already discussed, such as hyggebukser (hygge-pants), hyggelig (hygge-like), and hyggekrog (hygge-corner). In this way, the term 'comfort food' serves the very same function. The second way that comfort food reflects the tradition of hygge is comfort foods are particular to an individual, so not everyone will find comfort in the same foods. While these foods can differ from person to person, certain common denominators keep the various choices within the same category. One such common denominator is the simplicity of the food itself. Comfort food often includes pizza, pasta, or a bag of chips with dip—all things that are easy to make and equally easy to eat. They also tend to be hearty and unhealthy. Therefore, comfort foods aren't usually foods you can indulge in each and every day.

Again, if you were to ask for a single word to describe the feeling that eating pasta evokes, you would get many different answers. Some might say that it feels "homey," especially if they grew up in a home where their parents made pasta often. Others might say it feels "cozy" due to the warmth of the food. While all of these descriptions may be true, they aren't necessarily interchangeable. The inability to find a single word to express the feeling that a bowl of pasta creates comes from the same problem of trying to find one word that expresses the essence of hygge—it means something different for each and every person. Also, every person treats their pasta differently. Some will put salt and chili flakes on theirs. Some will put a mountain of cheese on it, whereas others will use little or no cheese. The experience of eating pasta has choices much like hygge does. No matter how you may eat your pasta, the complexity of the emotion experienced makes it challenging to define in a single word, much like the tea example used earlier in this chapter. That said, the word "comfort" is perhaps one word that can be used to define the essence of hygge. However, rather than searching for that elusive word, it might be best to say that hygge is like eating a bowl of pasta, making perfect sense to anyone who feels in their heart and mind that pasta is a comfort food.

Herein lies another way in which comfort food is a perfect example of hygge. While pasta might be comfort food for some, it may not make the list for others. Instead, they may see things like chips as comfort food. What makes a particular thing a comfort food isn't the food itself. Instead, it is the feeling that the food evokes in the individual. It is up to the individual to find out which foods create the desired result. For some, it may be warm foods such as oatmeal, pancakes, or the like. For others, it might be foods like cheese and crackers or popcorn. The fact that popcorn is fun to make can make it a perfect candidate for comfort food. When you make it in the pan, you get to watch and hear the "pop" of your ensuing snack. Popcorn can evoke true indulgence. You can put salt on it, sugar, cheese—anything that makes it comforting. It can also be paired with your favorite movie and evoke the nostalgia of going to the cinema with family. And maybe you don't even enjoy popcorn, and that's okay. It means there's more for the rest of us!

Perhaps the most outstanding example of hygge that has shifted into Western society's popular consciousness is one that has faced a similar linguistic challenge as hygge—the concept of Zen. What the term "Zen" has come to mean in Western culture is something completely different from what it means in its original East Asian cultural context. In the East, Zen is nothing more than a person's seated position when they are meditating. The word itself is an abbreviation of the word 'Zazen.' In essence, you can think of the term Zen as another word for "cross-legged." With this in mind, you begin to see how the term has come to mean something altogether different in the West than it does in the East. After all, how can you have a "cross-legged" mindset? How can the fragrance of a candle be considered "cross-legged"? Yet in the West, we use "Zen" to describe mindsets, atmospheres, responses to stress, and yes, even candle scents. This is because the lifestyle of those who practiced Zen meditation became something that Westerners began to crave, specifically the idea of transcending stress, negativity, and fear—things that are all too common in Western society. Thus, the term Zen was then used as a single word description for the results of meditation, not the meditation itself. Now the term has taken on such nebulous meaning that most people are wholly unaware of its origins.

Another aspect of Western Zen that reflects hygge is its focus on simplicity. Enjoying a walk through the woods or across the beach is considered Zen. Not only does it help a person reconnect with nature, but it can also lead to a state of peace and happiness without the need to use or purchase objects. Merely being content with what you have is a fundamental premise of Western Zen, and this ideal is also an integral part of the hygge culture too. More and more people are becoming aware of the fact that materialism doesn't bring the happiness that the societies we live in promise. Instead, materialism creates an insatiable hunger for acquiring more and is self-reinforcing. While each possession may provide happiness for a while, that happiness is fleeting, giving way to the desire to acquire yet more objects to provide that quick-fix of fleeting happiness. It's like a dog chasing its own tail on a societal level. Doing away with boundless materialism is where Zen can be most useful. Instead of finding pleasure in acquiring objects, Zen focuses on finding pleasure in the simple things in life. Again, these things' exact nature differs from person to person, just as it does in hygge. The important thing is that each individual finds those simple things that can bring them real and lasting happiness, and this "thing" will likely extend beyond getting the newest something-or-other.

In many ways, Zen's Western concept isn't altogether that much different from the concept of hygge. A Zen place is a place of peace and tranquility. Likewise, a Zen mindset is a frame of mind accepting events and circumstances that allow for serenity and calm. When a person has a Zen attitude, they don't allow themselves to be affected by criticism, anger, or other negative emotions, either from others or within. While these things may not seem to reflect the "cozy" nature of hygge, they do represent the aim of hygge, which is to restore peace and equilibrium to the heart and mind of the individual. Thus, the two concepts are closely related, even though they are different manifestations of the same principle. What makes this so essential is the fact that Zen has become such an influential part of Western culture, even though it is an entirely different entity from the original concept of Zazen. The Western tradition of Zen as the desire to achieve inner peace and harmony reflects a desire to abandon the fast-paced, cutthroat competitive paradigm of Western society. This same desire creates fertile ground in the West for hygge to take root and thrive.

The fact that the word "Zen" is used to describe a variety of different things demonstrates that no other single word can achieve that goal. There simply isn't a word in the English language that can adequately define the feeling or the experience of Zen. Rather than striving to find a replacement word, Zen merely got adopted as a term and acquired new definitions and purposes. While some might see this as sacrilege against Zen's original concept, the fact is that it represents a need within Western culture for something lacking.

That is, until now. The culture of hygge is in many ways equivalent to the Western idea of Zen, albeit without the same spiritual connotations. While yoga and meditation aren't necessarily required for hygge, they can certainly help inspire it. Thus, rather than trying to find alternate words to describe hygge and what it means, it probably would be best for Western society to simply adopt the word much the way it adopted the word 'Zen.' Then, instead of trying to explain hygge, people can simply recognize the hygge concepts they are already familiar with and begin to incorporate them into their lives in a more meaningful way. And with that, we can fully explore what hygge can do for an individual.

CHAPTER 12:

THE IMPACT OF HYGGE ON THE INDIVIDUAL

When a person develops a hygge lifestyle, they will discover many benefits manifesting in their life. We addressed some of these benefits in previous chapters, such as a marked decrease in stress and anxiety, which profoundly impacts a person's physical and mental well-being. However, there are additional benefits that will have just as profound an impact on a person's day-to-day life as the result of living a life-

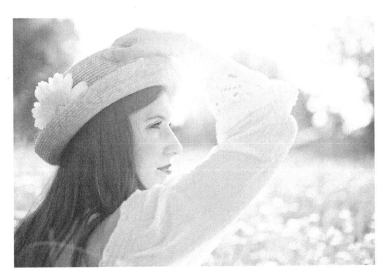

style in tune with hygge principles. Some of these benefits are a direct consequence of hygge, whereas others are more of an indirect consequence due to the changes made by hygge living. Whether direct or indirect, the one thing that all of these benefits have in common is that they are monumentally positive. This means that hygge is more than a feel-good practice. Hygge is a way of improving your life in a meaningful and results-driven way. The fact is that hygge can bring about positive changes in physical health, mental health, general well-being, relationships, performance at work, and even financial stability. In the end, when you ensure that hygge is second nature, all other aspects of your life will fall into place, which will provide you with the stability and freedom that few other lifestyles can offer.

The fact that hygge can improve a person's physical and mental health and well-being is relatively obvious to anyone who implements the hygge lifestyle. However, because it can also help improve a person's financial well-being is less obvious. Yet, this is a genuine and significant part of the impact that hygge can have on an individual. An easy way to portray the financial impact of hygge is to draw a comparison between hygge and another Western tradition that has hygge-like qualities—minimalism. The tradition of minimalism is similar to hygge in that it focuses on a person's quality of life in terms of experience rather than possessions. Doing away with needless possessions, which are often seen as "objects of attachment" by minimalists, is one of the goals of minimalism. As discussed, one of the defining aspects of modern Western culture is materialism. This manifests in the hyper-consumerist nature of industrialized societies. Unfortunately, the joy and lasting happiness that are promised once material goods are purchased perish after some short-term gratification. In other words, the end result is a brief high, followed by a crash, much like what you would experience if you ate a piece of cake for lunch. Just as you would be left hungry after a brief energy buzz and require more sustaining food for after you ate the cake, you too are left hungry for more products once the high has worn off from your last purchase.

Minimalism, like the hygge lifestyle, recognizes that this vicious cycle is not only self-defeating, but it is also extremely dangerous. After all, it is the constant craving for that temporary high that leads millions of people into crushing levels of debt year after year, something which minimalism can help alleviate. In an attempt to free people from the consumerist mindset, minimalism encourages people to find joy in everyday activities. Again, minimalists work to shift the focus away from the unbounded promises delivered by capitalism. When a person is able to find happiness in simple pleasures, they no longer need to purchase objects to satiate their craving for fulfillment. Instead, they can maintain happiness in a very real and lasting way, just as a person can maintain energy levels by eating healthier foods. This breaks the addictive cycle of hyper-consumerism, thereby improving a person's overall state of well-being. Since the hygge mindset focuses on enjoying life's simple pleasures, just like minimalism, it offers many of the same benefits. With hygge, you will realize that life is measured in the number and quality of experiences you have, not the number of things you own.

Replacing one's focus or dependence on consumer goods is where hygge can positively impact a person's financial well-being. Every year, we all spend money on goods that we don't need. We continuously buy these things because we are promised a great deal of happiness if we purchase a particular product. Unfortunately, this promise usually falls short, resulting in another purchase to experience the same fleeting high. However, we can break this seemingly endless cycle by following the hygge tradition. By finding happiness in life's simple pleasures through hygge techniques, people can free themselves from constantly spending money when they don't need to. Once you start finding happiness in the things you already have and in the places you already go, you will no longer need to keep spending more money to be happy. Not only will this happiness be more satisfying and long-lasting, but it will also keep you from going into debt as a result of buying product after product, chasing after the empty promises pushed by creative advertising campaigns. Therefore, when you begin to follow a hygge lifestyle, you will be able to save a considerable amount of money and use that money to bring better experiences into your life, thereby improving your life in a way that you most likely would not have expected otherwise.

Another way that hygge can significantly improve a person's life is in terms of personal relationships. All too often, people find themselves wishing that they could spend time with friends and family, if only they had more time available. This is the problem with continually focusing on work instead of the things that make up the rest of a person's life. One thing that hygge promotes is a change of priorities. When you begin to practice hygge, you will start to spend less time running the proverbial 'rat race' and more time on the things that truly matter. Once you slow down, you will free up valuable time that you can then spend with the special people in your life. You will no longer have to lose touch with the people close to your heart. Needless to say, this will improve your relationships by giving them much-needed attention. The problem with neglected relationships is that no matter how much people may mean to you, the relationship can become stale. This can result in feelings of estrangement and isolation, which can not only ruin a relation-ship, but can also have devastating effects on your emotional health and well-being.

Herein lies another considerable benefit that hygge can pro-vide—an improved state of mental and emotional well-being. When people become estranged from family and friends due to not having enough time to spend together, they can begin to feel isolated and alone. The more a person feels isolated and alone, the bigger life's problems can become to them. When you can talk to other people about day-to-day issues, you can face those issues with greater confidence. Not only are you able to get the stress and anxiety off your chest, but by talking things over, you might also be able to get advice and insight that can help you solve your dilemmas. Of course, this isn't a direct aspect of hygge, in the sense that the hygge lifestyle isn't about solv-ing life's problems. However, by spending more time with other people, you can avoid the feeling of having to face life alone, and this can make all the difference in the world. When you have friends and family close by, and you foster positive and en-riched experiences with these people, you will never feel alone. The emotional support that their presence alone provides can be invaluable in terms of being able to cope with difficult events. Thus, the togetherness that hygge promotes can have significant and authentic effects on stress reduction and emotional stability. These values are vital for surviving the fast-paced culture of Western society. Plus, you might find spending time with loved ones to be hygge in and of itself, so you can achieve goals you set out for your hygge lifestyle by being close to those that matter.

Another indirect benefit of hygge is that it can actually im-prove your performance at work. This may seem like a bit of a stretch at first, but hygge has the potential to improve every single facet of a person's life. Remember, in a previous chapter, we discussed how you could make your workplace more hygge? Well, implementing hygge can increase your performance at work, and the reason for it is quite simple. When you practice hygge in your day-to-day life, you will begin to reduce your general anxiety levels. Since stress and anxiety undermine your ability to perform to your full potential—at work and in other areas of life—and you reduce these by implementing hygge, your performance levels will increase.

Furthermore, by reducing your general levels of stress and anxiety, you will find that you can deal with day-to-day stresses at work more effectively. When your mindset is calm and more relaxed to start with, challenging days at work won't be as stressful as they were before. Therefore, by practicing hygge day to day, you can put yourself in a healthier and stronger frame of mind that will enable you to handle your work more effectively. When you handle work more effectively, you will likely come home in a better mood. Ensuring that you implement hygge at work not only affects who you are and how you feel at work but also all other aspects of your life. Work-life, home life, family life, and everything else are symbiotic. Never forget this.

Remember that it's a myth that hygge can only be experienced in specific environments; we do not need to fall prey to Western society's desire to compartmentalize things. Hygge doesn't require a particular home or outdoor environment; it is all dependent on the mindset. You can maintain that mindset wherever you are, no matter what you're doing, and regardless of the 'things' around you.

A perfect example of this truth can be found in a standard laundromat in Copenhagen. If you go to a laundromat in the U.S., you might be lucky enough to find a TV, or maybe a video game or two. However, this is far from guaranteed. Alternatively, in Copenhagen, you can find laundromats that have cafes. Now, rather than dividing your time up in terms of chores and time for yourself, you can combine the two. While doing laundry is a chore, it doesn't have to be a dreaded chore. Instead, people in Copenhagen sip hot drinks and eat delicious food while their clothes are spun clean. Anyone would be happy to do laundry with laundromats like that! And that's the point. Hygge isn't about escaping the mundane or obligatory aspects of life. Instead, it's about bringing joy and pleasure to those aspects. Few things could exemplify this way of thinking better than a café in a laundromat. Wherever you are, whatever you are doing, hygge can always be found or conjured up there. And when everyone engages in activities they may not like but finds a way to enjoy them anyway, society in general can be positively impacted.

CHAPTER 13:

THE IMPACT OF HYGGE ON SOCIETY

I f hygge can significantly impact an individual, then it can also impact society. After all, society is made up of individuals; therefore, anything that affects many individuals will—by nature—also affect society. Hygge is no exception to this rippling. As mentioned earlier in this book, Denmark has a long-standing tradition of ranking in the top three countries in the world in terms of overall happiness, and it is not a coincidence. After all, one might expect Denmark to rank far lower on the charts due to a plethora of social and environmental factors. For starters, the weather in Denmark is darker and colder than in most other countries. These conditions tend to worsen depression and anxiety rather than generate happiness.

Additionally, Denmark does not have a booming consumerist society—you won't find endless shopping malls and other places to buy the latest and greatest gadgets like you will in the UK or the US. Nor will you find a Hollywood scene of celebrities that take up significant space in the consciousness of the Danish populace to escape their day-to-day stresses. Yet, despite all of these factors, Denmark consistently ranks among the top three countries in terms of happiness, reaching the number one spot as often as not. Can hygge really be the reason behind this sustained happiness? In short, yes, it can. And I'm going to discuss with you why.

To understand how hygge improves an entire society's happiness, we must first examine the things that hygge replaces. We have already mentioned the vicious cycle of consumerism. No object can ever bring true happiness and satisfaction; it is experiences that bring authentic joy to a person's life. That is why hygge is so effective at establishing and maintaining happiness, not only on the individual level but also on the social level. By focusing on experience rather than possessions, hygge can rescue a person from the endless cycle of consumerism and restore a genuine sense of happiness and contentment. However, this is only possible when someone begins to appreciate the simple pleasures in life. When most individuals in a community share this experience of appreciation, it begins to shape the social dynamic in an authentic way. Now, instead of streets full of people who are stressed out and eager to get their next consumer "fix," you have streets full of people who enjoy day-to-day life and understand and appreciate the things that are truly important in life. You will see streets where people move around more slowly, are less stressed and are focused on what they are doing rather than on the next thing.

As bad as the emptiness and inadequacy many people experience due to consumerism is, this way of living is only half of the problem. The other half of the problem is the crushing debt that so many people accrue in their attempts to fill their lives with the products and services that promise to bring them the happiness they crave. It is no secret that the economies in the West are debt-based, meaning that most people have debts rather than savings. Thus, not only does consumerism cause a sense of inadequacy and a sense of unfulfillment, but it also destroys the financial security that most people work so hard to achieve. Now, instead of a bank account full of retirement savings, the average Westerner has a storage shed full of unwanted and un-used items that will never provide the joy and happiness that the consumerist world promised to them. Having all this stuff results in nothing but stress and anxiety, and the very real feeling that you do not have the money to get the things you need but cannot afford and a home full of clutter and junk. Danish people don't tend to waste their money on needless junk that only takes up space, and it wouldn't be incorrect to attribute this phenom-enon to the hygge lifestyle. Instead, Danes tend to spend a larger portion of their money on quality time with friends, family, and loved ones. This quality time brings the joy and fulfillment that consumerism promises yet always fails to deliver. As a result, the average Dane has a contented heart and a solvent bank account, meaning that their financial stress levels are all but non-existent compared to those in consumerist societies.

Let it be known that I do not want to minimize the debt many people fall into, even if they live modestly possessions-wise. There are expensive mortgages, car payments, and colossal student loan debt in the USA and many other countries. However, my point is that so many of us still purchase things we either do not need or cannot afford, leading to further stress, anxiety, and financial hardship. Hey, maybe a hygge activity could be selling all the stuff you have but do not need or donating clothes you never wear to charities. Carrying out these activities would both lighten your load of material goods and either bring you some money or make you feel good that you are making a positive difference for others.

So, the impact that this economic security has on the individual is obvious, but how does this affect society as a whole? One significant difference between Danish society and American society is the amount of importance placed on work. Since the average Dane has all that they need to live a comfortable, happy, content life, they don't tend to have the desire to make more and more money, unlike many of their American counterparts. This attitude strongly affects how Danes view their work. Rather than centering their life and activities around work, Danish people tend to center on their whole lives and recognize that work merely comprises one aspect of it. They still have a schedule to work by, and they still have to work well in order to earn a paycheck. However, they don't tend to feel the need to be on standby 24 hours a day, seven days a week like so many Americans sadly are. Additionally, businesses aren't in such fierce competition with each other since the mentality of needing to be number one simply doesn't exist. Rather than needing to be the best, businesses recognize the importance of being a part of a greater whole, and their CEOs recognize they occupy a symbiotic place as just one part of the human world.

Being a part of the greater whole is a fundamental aspect of hygge in itself. By focusing on family and loved ones, the individual rediscovers their place in the grand scheme of things. Individual success and dominance will no longer be a way of life, and instead, cooperation, togetherness, and a sense of collective well-being take root. Thus, the stress and anxiety of always needing to be number one are entirely removed, replaced by a sense of satisfaction and gratitude for life in general. This permeates every level of society, shaping such things as work/life balance, political accountability, and even fiscal responsibility.

Another way in which hygge positively impacts society as a whole is that, by eliminating hyper-consumerism, it significantly reduces the waste we create—to the benefit of the planet we all call home. While consumerist societies can boast of substantial production numbers and sales figures, they have to also admit to overwhelming amounts of waste. Some of this waste is the result of more items being produced than are purchased. However, the vast majority of it results from perfectly good items being discarded to make room for the latest and greatest 'stuff' available. More and more electronics, clothing, automobiles, and other items are discarded year after year for no other reason than they simply aren't chic or up-to-date enough. The fact that they are in perfect working order never seems to matter at all. This rampant degree of waste only serves to compound our ever-present environmental nightmare. After all, where do you begin to put things that simply won't decompose over the course of time? Plastics, glass, metal components, and other parts constructed from non-biodegradable materials are what are used to create countless electronic items such as smartphones, computers, and tablets. Subsequently, when a phone is thrown away, it will take up space for hundreds if not thousands of years. Multiply that by millions of people per year, and you have yet another contribution to environmental disaster. And this environmental catastrophe is where a societal hygge mindset comes to the rescue yet again.

Since hygge takes the focus off consumerism, the average person living hygge will use a phone, laptop, and the like until they are no longer functioning. When you multiply this by the number of people in society, you could reduce overall waste production exponentially. After all, instead of buying a new phone each year, or even worse, every few months, the average Dane will buy a new phone every three to five years or more. The same goes for every other electronic device that they own. Chances are, the average Dane doesn't own as many electronic components to start with, since they don't see the same need for them. This means that Denmark's environment is far safer and cleaner because non-biodegradable trash has been limited significantly.

Hygge can have several other positive effects on a society's environment. First and foremost is a reduction in carbon emissions. Since activities such as walking and bicycling are often considered hygge, the amount of pollution caused by driving cars is significantly reduced in a hygge society. There's less need to own a car in a place like Denmark. When walking and bicycling are seen as viable alternatives to driving, even people who own cars will drive them less and keep the same one longer. This helps to keep the air considerably cleaner. Fewer cars also mean that fewer roads are required, meaning fewer disruptive construction projects. Additionally, fewer cars mean fewer parking lots are needed, which keeps the rural and urban landscapes far more visually appealing.

Another way that hygge helps the environment is to create a greater sense of appreciation for one's surroundings. When people take the time to enjoy a walk in the woods, they will be a lot less likely to cut the forest down in order to build a new shopping complex. Furthermore, when people find happiness and pleasure in their surroundings, they also tend to care for those surroundings better. Litter, pollution, over-development, and other harmful acts against nature are not accepted in hygge societies. Not only does this create an environment that is more harmonious with nature, but one that is healthier for people and all living things. Nature reduces stress and anxiety. Therefore, a nature-friendly environment will also be relaxing and calming for anyone living there.

Furthermore, the physical health benefits of a nature-friendly environment are highly significant. Better air quality, reduced noise pollution, and cleaner water are all abundant in places that protect and appreciate nature. Thus, when a society takes on a hygge approach to life, the symbiotic relationship between humanity and nature is maintained or restored.

Finally, there is the impact of hygge on crime and social disorder. While crime will exist in every society to some degree, crime rates are much lower in societies where hygge is a normal way of life. This is particularly true in the case of violent crime. Studies have shown that stress, anxiety, and the feeling of isolation and being alone are significant factors that contribute to crime in all forms, but especially violent crime. That said, it stands to reason that any society where a hygge lifestyle reduces these factors will have a significantly lower rate of crime as a result. Not only is crime lower in Denmark overall, but violent crime is all but non-existent compared to what it is in non-hygge Western societies. The importance of reducing stress and increasing life-satisfaction in an individual cannot be over-stated. Any person who is generally happier with life will be far less likely to break any laws, as they will have less motivation to do so. When you take that to the social level, the numbers speak for themselves. In terms of non-violent crimes, Denmark ranks between 10th and 25th in the world, depending on the specific crime. In terms of violent crimes, Denmark ranks as low as 104th in the world. The vast spread between being in the top three happiest countries and being 104th for violent crime is no coincidence. It is a direct consequence of hygge being practiced on a societal and national level. And, once a society and a country are as hygge as possible, that can affect the entire world.

CHAPTER 14:

THE IMPACT OF HYGGE ON THE WORLD

So far, we have learned about the impact of hygge on the individual and an entire society. Since society comprises of individuals, if hygge can increase an individual's happiness, and most people in a given society practice hygge, then it could be assumed that a particular society would become happier in general. We have also seen how hygge can affect other aspects of society as well, including financial stability, environmental well-being, and a whole host of other critical measures. If a society is happier, then the world is that much happier. If a society can spread its positive way of life to other societies, the world will be even happier! Therefore, it is beyond dispute that hygge has a real impact on both an individual level and a collective level. The only question left to answer is just how far the effects of hygge can reach. If hygge can improve a person's life and a society, can it also improve the world at large? Can hygge provide the answers that humanity so desperately needs at this vital moment of human history? Based on what we have discovered so far, the answer to that question is a resounding "yes." After all, just as society is made up of a large number of individuals, so too, the world is made up of a large number of societies. Therefore, if the impact of hygge on the individual can influence society, then the impact of hygge on society should be able to influence the world. That influence could, in fact, be the very thing that humanity needs in order to restore peace and prosperity to a world suffering in turmoil. Therefore, it is essential to recognize yourself as one of the pieces in the sizeable hygge puzzle. By implementing hygge, you become that much more of a positive influence on the world around you.

In order to understand the changes that hygge could bring to the world, it is essential first to understand the problems that the world currently struggles with. If you were to ask the average person what one thing they would change about the world if they had a magic wand, the chances are most would eliminate war. War has dominated human history, and it has only gotten worse due to sophisticated weaponry. The 20th century saw the deadliest conflicts the world had ever seen, and over 108 million people died due to conflict in this 100-year span. Every corner of the world is caught up in a conflict of one size or another even right now. This state of war is the antithesis of the serene and peaceful environment that hygge can create and the harmony that the lifestyle promises. Just as hygge can help a single person remove stress and anxiety from their life, and thus live a life of inner and outer peace, hygge could also remove much of the hatred and strife that causes nations and groups to go to war with each other in the first place. After all, one of the main aspects of hygge is the quest for pleasure and comfort. When an individual seeks out happy moments, not only do they find happiness and thus relieve stress, but they also change their outlook on life in general. Rather than looking for reasons to complain or start a fight, a person practicing hygge will look for opportunities to be happy and experience comfort. Anyone looking to be happy will be far less likely to engage in a conflict of any sort. When you multiply this to the collective world level, this would mean that countries would spend their time and energy on finding pleasure and contentment rather than trying to dominate and control the rest of the planet. Any country that spent its resources searching for ways for its entire population to be comfortable and happy would totally oppose anything that would stand in the way of that ideal. Since war and conflict would undermine the happiness (and fun) the people in a country could experience, it makes sense that a country practicing hygge would strongly avoid anything that would lead to war or conflict. Needless to say, that would be a far different reality than the one we face in the world today. However, as individuals, it is up to us to change that and bring more peace to the world at large.

In fact, we can easily draw a correlation between war and the overall focus of a nation, specifically its cultural value system. Throughout history, it is a common theme that nations that fixated on depriving themselves of worldly pleasures were far more likely to engage in a global conflict in one form or another. This is likely due to the suppression of their desires, which leads to an inner conflict, which is then projected onto the outside world. Sometimes this conflict would take the shape of an actual war with another developed nation, such as wars between Britain and France, or Britain and Spain, whereas other times, this conflict would take the shape of wars of conquest, such as the Spanish conquest of the New World. This trend is also evident in more recent times, such as in World War II. When you examine Germany and Japan's cultural values, you see the common thread of leaving behind a certain level of worldly pleasure for devotion to duty and service to the state. The idea wasn't to find happiness in life but rather to promote nationalism and racial supremacy. This fixation on national identity, specifically as being superior to other nations and races, gave rise to the justification for fighting wars of conquest and subjugation over the supposedly 'inferior' peoples of Earth. Rather than being an isolated incident, this direct relationship between sacrifice and violence can be seen throughout human history. Therefore, in the way that a certain mindset can bring about conflict, war, and strife, another mindset can bring about peace, love, and harmony. If people and nations in the 20th century were more focused on the wellbeing of all through a hygge mindset, maybe everything would have been different. But that wasn't the reality. However, we all have a chance to make things better for the world today by changing our mindsets as individuals.

In contrast to early- and mid-20th century Germany and Japan, you can look at nations that focus on finding pleasure and joy in life and will find cultures that are far less willing to engage in a war of any kind. It is of little wonder that the Scandinavian countries, specifically Denmark, have been off the radar in terms of global conflicts for a considerable length of time. While some might argue that Denmark's size is what keeps them from being a global threat, it would be worth pointing out that Great Britain, the Netherlands, and Japan are not too dissimilar in terms of size. Yet, all of these countries have involved themselves in numerous global conflicts over the past few centuries. When it comes to war, one simple rule of thumb prevails—"Where there's a will, there's a way." The size of a nation doesn't necessarily dictate whether or not that nation will be capable of waging war on another. Rather, the heart of a nation determines that. It also goes with the consumerist mindset that some countries wage war. They want more: more riches, more territories, and more influence on the global stage. For example at its peak, the British Empire ruled more than 1/3 of the world—to do so requires a level of war-waging and subjecting other people to their rule. They were focused on expansion and conquest, not peace for all. Thus, countries that focus on finding happiness and peace in day-to-day life, regardless of size, are the ones that will avoid conflict at virtually all costs.

Denmark is a good example. Its current status as the seat of hygge—much like Tibet is the seat of Buddhism—means that the nation as a whole has absolutely no interest in causing harm or suffering, either to its own people or the other people in the world at large. It is the prime example of a nation embracing peace and happiness. Again, they are focused on experience, no accumulating more land or things.

Just to drive the point home in a way that might be easier to measure, consider the fact that Denmark was one of the countries of origin for the infamous Vikings, who engaged in global warfare of various forms several centuries ago. They engaged in nefarious war practices—like pillaging villages—and they were also interested in power, control, and dominance. The fact that the same country that helped create the Viking culture also launched the hygge culture shows just how significant the hygge lifestyle is in transforming a society and a people. After all, Denmark is a modern-day beacon of happiness and peace, a far cry from their reputation in the ninth century. Now, rather than being the nation of ruthless, blood-thirsty warriors wielding swords and axes, Denmark is a nation of happiness, pleasure, and warmth (the people, not the climate!).

The reason the Danes are synonymous with these things alongside the rise in popularity of the hygge tradition is no mere coincidence. Rather, it demonstrates the very real correlation between hygge and the national identity of 21st century Denmark. Imagine, if one country can reinvent itself through adoption of hygge, how different the world could become if every country were to do the same? If instead of trying to be the best and trying to dominate others, countries would simply seek for their citizens pleasure in day-to-day life—all war, turmoil, and strife could come to an end. If we were to create peace and harmony in our own lives, how transformative could these practices improve others' lives?

Hygge could also help eliminate various other threats to the world in general. One such threat is the destruction of the environment. While there are several reasons the planet is undergoing environmental challenges of different forms, humankind's exploitation of minerals and other natural resources is perhaps the most significant. It is certainly the most controllable, and the one that would be directly impacted if the world as a whole started practicing hygge. Since hygge reduces the influence of materialism and consumerism, it makes sense that if the world followed the hygge way of life, then the need to extract minerals and raw materials would decrease exponentially.

Furthermore, the excess waste dumped into landfills would be reduced, resulting in the environment being protected 'at both ends' of the production-to-dumping lifecycle. Not only would the environment not be depleted of resources, but it would also not be a dumping ground for humanity's trash. Unfortunately, since many countries remain rooted in hyper-consumerism, it seems that the environment is a long way from being cared for the way that it both deserves and needs. However, you only have to look at countries like Denmark, where consumerism is not the way of life, to see how the environment could be improved if more of the world took on the lifestyle of hygge. Through the actions of each of us reducing our focus on material goods, we could help the environment monumentally. Exchanging consumerist goods for experiences may just be the step we need to take to save the planet.

Another way the environment would benefit from hygge is that humanity would stop treating it as unimportant, and perhaps more as a single, living organism or ecosystem. The number one reason so many industries continue to dump waste and toxic materials into the rivers and oceans is that they simply have lost all sense of respect and admiration for nature. Profit and short-cuts are the sole focus of many corporations that neglect to consider the damage done to the planet. But since hygge promotes spending time in nature in order to find peace and happiness, it ultimately fosters a greater love and appreciation for nature. The result will be a more symbiotic relationship between humankind and the environment, which will lead to a new appreciation of the natural world. When this relationship is restored, then the abuses against nature and the environment will come to an end.

No person or entity that appreciates nature would continue to poison the rivers and oceans with waste material.

Additionally, the need for oil and gas would be reduced exponentially as more and more people began to use less intrusive forms of transportation than those requiring fossil fuels. Not only would this help protect the environment from constant drilling and mining, but it would also help clean the air of the carbon gasses that are causing all sorts of environmental problems. Whether you accept the science or not, the fact is that the climate on this planet is changing. If more of the world would respect and protect nature, as the hygge lifestyle encourages, then it is possible that this threat could be stopped before it is too late. We are near the point of no return, so we must act now to not step over the line. There is so little time, so immediate action is imperative.

Finally, there is the impact that hygge could have on things such as famine, disease, and other such dangers that threaten the lives of millions. While hygge isn't necessarily rooted in helping other people—although it can be for you—it does help foster a greater sense of community. This is particularly true in terms of family. By spending more time with family and friends, a person can hardly turn a blind eye to when members of their inner circle are struggling in life. It makes sense that as your friends and family become more important to you that you would want to help them whenever possible. Again, this isn't necessarily a direct goal of hygge, but it is a very real side effect of practicing a hygge lifestyle. If this attitude were taken to a global level, nations worldwide would put forth a greater effort to lend assistance to places hit by famine, disease, and natural disasters. Rather than making a token effort for appearance's sake, countries would strive to solve the problems and bring lasting relief to those affected. This would be a global manifestation of the hygge sense of family and community. By embracing every nation as a part of the global family, no country would be able to stand by idly while the populace of another nation suffered and died.

Furthermore, since consumerism and greed are replaced by generosity and gratitude through hygge, it makes sense that each nation's leaders and citizens would find joy in healing the planet. Instead of using humanitarian efforts to exert political leverage, nations would use them to increase all people's happiness and contentment. All in all, hygge could turn the world into a place where humanity respects nature, preserves peace, and promotes happiness and well-being for all people and life on planet Earth.

CONCLUSION

W hen it comes to defining, categorizing, and identifying a feeling of hygge, the term "lifestyle" does not quite capture it. With many lifestyles, there are certain rules, strategies, practices, and mantras. Hygge, however, does not encompass rules, regulations, products, or even stereotypical mantras. It encompasses a *feeling*. This is the reason the Scandinavian word is untranslatable in many countries. For areas of the world that base their ideas of success, wealth, and growth on personal assets and analyzed statistics, the idea of utilizing emotion to somehow judge personal growth on these scales is foreign and nonsensical. In many countries and cultures, the amount of land one owns or even the amount of money in the bank is how success in life is measured.

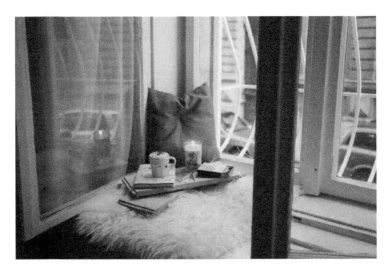

Not so with some cultures, especially the Danish culture, but also the Nordic culture at large. That is the difference.

So, how do you take a word that points to a completely different ruler of measurement for success and define it in a culture that sees that same ruler as a foreign concept?

It's easy: you simply promote the idea of self-awareness.

Being self-aware in the lifestyle of hygge is essential, especially for those raised in a culture in which emotion is something to cast off to the side in favor of other things (or a 'stiff upper lip,' as the British call it). For those raised in cultures where emotion and feelings are even considered one's downfall, the lifestyle of hygge can be almost impossible to understand, much less promote.

But to people in these types of cultures, hygge can be the most freeing and healthy lifestyle they can choose to live. If individuals in these cultures shift their mindsets, they may plant the seeds of a more open society.

Hygge is not merely the promotion of relaxation and comfort, though that is how one gauges whether or not hygge is being achieved. Promoting these aspects of life enable inward health, from physical healing to mental rejuvenation. The reduction of stresses and anxieties helps the body heal from the damage that stress induces over long periods of time. Stress reduction reduces levels of damaging chemicals, which can elicit everything from life-threatening fatigue to chronic, debilitating migraines. Allowing the body to relax enables organs to filter the cortisol from the bloodstream and muscle tissue so that automatic immune responses can kick into overdrive and begin to repair the body.

Reducing stress and anxieties also promotes mental health. Many cases of depression, including the seasonal variety, can be traced back to an overflow of cortisol in the body, specifically for those who suffer from chronic migraines that create lesions in the brain that hamper neurotransmitter receptors. Lesions prevent those synapses and neurons from absorbing the chemicals the brain needs to balance itself. This imbalance results in a slew of issues because of an overload of cortisol in response to constant stressors.

Emotional health is also impacted positively by a hygge lifestyle. All of these issues that stem from debilitated physical and mental health ultimately affect someone emotionally. Chemical imbalances can create mood swings that lead to mounting self-consciousness, anxiety, and panic attacks. These attacks promote more bodily harm, which in turn causes a negative reel of thoughts to play out repeatedly in someone's head, and the cyclical process ultimately destroys all three facets of personal health. This happens all because of a chronic surge of cortisol in their systems.

Hygge is driven by one guideline and one guideline alone: "Treat yourself with kindness." In a world where people are constantly distracted with things that seem more important than their overall health, it is hard to convey the importance of recognizing that you are the only one responsible for taking care of yourself. We all watch romantic lifetime movie marathons where one character is ultimately abusing themselves in some way until another character swoops in, recognizes all of their faults, throws themselves into fixing the other, and then they fall in love and live happily ever after. And while that is a popular romantic notion, it harbors an extremely dangerous message: that someone else will come along and take care of you eventually.

And most often, that is not the case.

Hygge is about self-care. Hygge promotes the idea of relaxation and the idea of being strong enough to take care of oneself. It promotes the foundation of putting yourself first and conceals it under a mask of "you deserve this." Not only do you deserve it, but you also are entitled to it, yet it is up to you to go out there and earn it. With the mounting stresses this life will ultimately dole out to every single person on this planet, you are entitled to downtime during which the only focus is on you. There is a reason why hair salons, spas, movie theaters, concerts, stage productions, and even some vacation packages can charge as much as they do and get away with it. They understand people's insatiable desire to relax and "get away from it all."

However, the idea that hundreds, or even thousands, of dollars need to be spent to achieve the experience of unwinding and relaxing is far from the truth. Media advertising campaigns have trained us to expect high prices depending on the level of relaxation and pampering we wish, and even those decisions can become stressful. The sheer amount of money spent can turn a relaxing vacation into yet another stressful event in someone's life.

That is not the type of relaxation hygge promotes.

Instead, hygge focuses on ordinary personal necessities and helps translate them into personal enjoyment exercises. If someone's innermost need is to sleep, then hygge suggests doing something like purchasing that comfortable pajama set you have been eyeballing or drinking a warm cup of tea before you retire for the night. If someone's innermost need is to stay warm during the winter, hygge promotes long, hot showers or baths and warm, comfortable blankets. Suppose someone's innermost need is to be around friends and partake in uproarious laughter. In that case, hygge promotes watching a comedy movie with friends or enjoying a glass of wine over a great conversation in a comfortable room. Hygge can be implemented at all times, anywhere, and fits any budget.

In other words, hygge does not promote spending money to relax; it promotes enhancing atmospheres already accessible to us that aid in relaxation.

For Danes, hygge is a natural necessity. Just as constantly being available for a job is common in many cultures, consistent hygge is common in Danish culture. Danes decorate their apartments, purchase their homes, and even arrange family events with the idea of hygge in mind. For many in the Danish culture, doing this type of thing is natural and requires little to no additional thought. It is why many Danes have just as hard a time explaining it as many cultures do understanding it: because it is so natural and ingrained, it is hard for them to understand that not everyone lives this way.

For example, if someone came up to you and asked you to define the word "living," what would you say? Perhaps someone has asked you what it means or how you do it... what would you tell them? Would you say that "living" means getting up and breathing? Or that "living" means going out and enjoying life? Or that "living" even means enjoying what life has to offer? If you ask ten different people, you will acquire ten different answers, and that is what would happen if you asked ten Danes to define the word "hygge."

You would get ten different answers, not because it is rare and misunderstood, but because it is common *and* personal.

When it comes down to it, hygge is a feeling generated by a particular surrounding based solely on the interpreter of the situation. What one person finds comforting, another will find annoying or bothersome. What one person finds idiotic, another might find funny. And what one person finds beautiful, another might find unattractive. Hygge incorporates just as much diversity as the people implementing the lifestyle, and that is the beauty of the entire concept: rules and regulations do not apply. Dollar amounts and income status do not apply. It is not confined to a specific country or race or gender, or sexual orientation. It is merely about how the person experiencing life interprets any particular experience emotionally.

That is what hygge truly is: a personal experience between yourself and relaxation.

All this lifestyle does is promote self-care in a way many people neglect. All this lifestyle promises is to make sure you are the healthiest you can be. All this lifestyle is about is to make you happy.

You do not work for this lifestyle; it works for you.

And that is its true, unadulterated beauty.

Welcome to the world of hygge. It's time to enjoy your new standard of living!

THANKS FOR READING

I really hope you enjoyed this book, and most of all, got more value from it than you had to give.

It would mean a lot to me if you left an Amazon review—I will reply to all questions asked!

Simply find this book on Amazon, scroll to the reviews section, and click "Write a customer review". Or please visit www.pristinepublish.com/hyggereview to leave a review

Be sure to check out my email list, as I will constantly share valuable knowledge with you.

The best way to get the list currently is by visiting www.pristinepublish.com/minimalist and entering your email.

Here, I'll provide actionable information that aims to improve your enjoyment of life.

I'll update you on my latest books and I'll even send free e-books that I think you'll find useful.

Kindest regards,

Olivia Telford